# POEMS
# FROM
# THREE
# DECADES

# POEMS FROM THREE DECADES

by Richmond Lattimore

Charles Scribner's Sons New York

To Alice again

# CONTENTS

## POEMS (1957)

## SESTINA FOR A FAR-OFF SUMMER

## THE STRIDE OF TIME

*[x]*

## NEW POEMS

*[xi]*

[xii]

# POEMS
# FROM
# THREE
# DECADES

# POEMS (1957)

## NORTH PHILADELPHIA TRENTON AND NEW YORK

Thin steel, in paired lines forever mated, cuts
forks and crosses, catches blue light, threads a station and a yard,
finds a bridge across the winter Schuylkill lithograph,
slips by the winter boardings, the chimney pots, the dirty
windowpanes and chimneys cut aslant for factories
either way aside.

          Now square your panes, look
large to wheel the brittle gray, the deep
horizon up. The prison steps into your square, and runs beside,
and drops away. The nunnery, the monastery after it,
fleetly shine, dip, recover, and are gone,
as houses in precise astonished rows come out,
sit up and solidify, stare, and are politely wheeled away.
Under bridge and under wheel the Delaware floats down
ice cakes, watched by the gilt glitter of the Capitol.

North now, sky change on earth angle altering,
color of iron blooms on spinneys, Breughel snow and brown tree
authenticate the high parallel.

          In North Jersey, flat, endlessly
arranged in silver gas cylinders, shine of plane wing, deep
dirty and deliberate rivers grope between meadows
where the catkins keep good order and the posters march beside you,
and the turnpike loping near on legs of pylons stays to race you,
and the hill with houses slides to meet you.

          The tunnel: you are gone,
and the bright winter sky as from a tube of indigo is squeezed away.

[1]

# GOOD SPEED FOR SOUTHWARD VOYAGERS

Now as you lose our sands, banks, fogs, and north,
may all Atlantic graces bless your prow
and progress forth;
Boreas sleep and bergs recede, gulls follow,
and all that's debonair at sea rise on your bow;

grave sister steamers salute with formal dip
of colors; wake-wings foam and murmur and submerge
behind your ship,
where dimly you discern at the far verge
some dripping Cytherea of the calms emerge.

Ah yes, may strange and benign sea monsters keep
you, and helmed, armed, and bosomy wind-cherubs, four
at the four corners of the deep,
bulging where blue is blue forevermore,
wave you with tridents to the Mediterranean shore.

*[2]*

# A LETTER TO TWELVE PEOPLE

Bring back the early summer when you come,
and nine o'clock, and the gray angles
of towers breaking gleams along wet cobbles,
and lamps spilling on tangles

of water plied like rope; and bring the night
kneeling quietly on Witham, and the strain
of ivy on the broken cloister, and bring
the drip of water, and the after-rain

stillness of thick trees sleeping in the stream
on their own quiet idols there; and you
will float these gifts along your path for me.
These are the things we knew:

a bridge, a weir, an inn, a fallen tree;
the wakening lights a net laid slack
on the gray city, and all that was held in these.
Bring them when you come back.

*[3]*

MID-CONTINENTAL

Here, stuck on a green and brown hillside,
confined only by soft clumps on skylines, mound
and fault; by high hawk-ridden air, the bright well whose purpling thunders
    bud and hide
the grown edge; by near walnuts green under dust; lapped in sound

of blond country summer; reaping noises, far dogs and cattle; rain
stepping hushed in distances; here in half-across, the self-spelled
and self-mirrored, the narcissus brain
labors to imagine beyond eyescape's small miles. Oh, we are held

and smeared like flies by water on the sticky wheel
of what we were and what we are. We dream
more than remember how, east and west, the tossed halves of the Ocean seal
the brown in blue; how dawn there crowds our noon, stars swim

before our sunset. But there still the sea moon pulls her black tides
and our big ball, set with water-queens heading the white-hilled
bulge, turns always; and always his grand downside
holds blue water close upon him, not pinned with rock or stanchion, no drop
    spilled.

[4]

# MARGINALS

To me lying near sleep, at the pale edge
of dark, sounds wrestle the gray beyond, and trains
at the outer margin slide and weave, the diesels
shudder their strings of cars and eat their noisy
miles, and farmlights star the black between.

To me lying near sleep the near leaves bind
my walls in hush of green gloom merged in still
and ebony and humming waves of leafed
midnight, where the small insect noises drown
in those deep currents that close in my walls.

To me lying near sleep the shuttered blinds
spill in a float of morning colors, wash
and rinse my eyes, disturb the escape of dreams
upon the white awakeness lying beside
my wakening in blithe birdsong and drenched day.

*[5]*

# SEARCH

The way a diver ropes
his pattern in the cool green
shadows woven in water
the arms develop
blue curves and puzzled arcs;
and the water torn above
gives his eyes to the sun
and the kneeling bay
and the white rocks drenched at the base
and the gazing ships;
and the arms design
their dripping action again
stroke and overstroke
the legs in foam blurred
driving weight in water.
In the sun on the wet planks
eyes and body
remember
the lit downgoing, and under
soft masses of water the wrist
ribboned in weed, the hard sand,
the armored crabs in the clefts,
seaferns in the rock-knees,
deserted wood of killed galleys,
a gold coin in the sand,
the still stare
forever
of the upward eyes trapped under
the lost keel.
So from the boards in the sun
recall
that underwater,
and the lumber left, and the dead men,
and their names, and the ships' names,
and the dead faces.

[6]

# SEA CHANGES

Not in one of its furies, but with absent care,
the slaty tide sucks bones of wood, spits them dry
on the sand; plasters a shell here, there
one derelict claw; brown weed ribbons (sea hair
waving submerged); pebble stuff, piled high.

Is it this thoughtful arranger, patting (now) a small splash
on sand, whose January angers boiled in whale-
battering shipless heaves of water, tall
in the gray gull-blown wind, to climb and crash
like a wet axe, and clobber and bruise our littoral?

Log it to commonplace that the sculpture of coast,
what sleeves and shapes the blue barrier either side,
is wild winter days blown monstrous, shaken slammed and lost;
with spelled calms, held water, carving slow and leaving uppermost
a decor of sea bones, shell spar net, displayed beyond high tide.

*[7]*

# NOT HAPPY NATURE, NOT UNHAPPY WE

*I do not fall upon the thorns of life.*
*I do not bleed.*


Wading in sand on the western edge, we saw
the continent bordered with fishermen,
surf-blown about the feet, their Japanese
strong legs shoved into hip boots, standing
all in a lonely line, behind whose sentinel and sea-
ward facing frieze the dunes
gave amorous escape to those hand-in-hand
couples that brushed the shrubs, and then were gone.
Our tactful eyes were also seaward. Some surprise
of light had torn the colors of the air,
or was it distance or illusion broke
the dragons of the skyscape Farallones
to fragments of mirage? Thunder-colored
on flame. Admirable. But the wind
blew in our bones.

And birds of the sea, what were they, all
necks and beaks, drove their bitter profiles across
the curtain of a storm where no storm was,
guided on rags of sea-lace, and went home,
wherever home can be for such.

                    And here, I thought
long afterward, watching the leafmen rake
and pile and burn the brown and bronze of Penn-
sylvanian oaks, and make their ordered lines of men
make the slow pensive motions that men make at work,
here, as I thought again, we should have grieved
for our sad souls amid the spirit world
of broken water and grave birds. We were not sad
but only cold.
Weltschmerz today can be no private thing.

Not our hurt, but only the hurt of a world
with a worm in its axis, a rotten old ball
whose progress may at any moment begin to wobble
perceptibly.

As for us, we sought to hide
behind the eucalyptus, whose abject leaves
thinned the water from the Pacific breeze
to drip on us.

Huddling, no more in love
than for mere heat, we saw the fishermen
march homeward through the valley of the dunes
in profiles of wet hats and slanted poles
and solemn ordered lines of men at work.

And now in time of leafsmoke, ankle-deep
in crackled old bronze, where they rake and burn,
think how it was in smoke, spume, spindrift clouding
to haze the standing continental shapes
that we forgot to grieve
for our sad souls, and not the cracking world.

*[9]*

# NOTE ON THE L & N

Bracketed by a diesel switcher and five
box cars before, and aft a red caboose,
with pistons pumping as if they were alive,
with eyeholes fixed ahead, cabhandles loose,
two old pacifics went
frogmarched to fate along the iron arc
that hooked the landscape to the edge of dark.

Dull on the wheels and ironed calm by time
the history of bright miles dies to the trip
of driving rods pushed from outside. They climb
in humped and prodded dead companionship
where the last curve is bent
and shapes them home. No more, in pride of steam,
will they thread out against the azure dream

of six o'clock on silver, past the sleep
of yards, the sleep of white grain towers, to raise
blue cities hours in future. Life is deep
dimmed in them, and their black is dull with days.
In a bewilderment
of motion they find aliens work their wheeled
stride to the scrapyard, and the ironmonger's field.

*[10]*

RMS *LUSITANIA*


Down under green,
under blown gray, white creaming
indigo across the collapse of slipping waterhills, thin
with wind hollowed through spray, gulls screaming,

under the cold still pool
of crosslit green that slabs the giant fidgeting skin of the world's ocean,
where water stilled, jelled, is nothing like water except to be cool,
and wears no color but color of silence after commotion;

there on the blind floor she has been lying
since the iron fish exploded in the heart,
since her short drama of dying,
sloped boats, hopeless swimmers, flame water steam shrieking her apart.

Big broken and black
she bulks there still in the gloom
with enormities of red keel, girded bridge and stack;
hulled gold (they said); paintings decor silver china; grace-ghosts of the
    stateroom, the dining room.

Lost? Saved? Sealed for judgment? Did you find
your islands there, your harbor and berth, green down
these miles, promised that day, that moment above in the sun, when your
    blind
and dying swimmers watched you drown?

*[11]*

## STEAM CROSSING: MIDWEST

Grass dries brown between rails.
Weeds crowd up through concrete slabs. A few
strung wires slant. The grain tower
shapes a white tube on the blue.

The Wooden Implement Store is padlocked.
Boards slat bare in the sun. Through cracks
bent blades, shovels and plows, tool
handles cross in sepia gloom. The tracks

define the blank front of town. Far
at the crossing, cars, bright new bugs, pick
a dainty way between gate arms. A single truck
careens, lurches near, one thick

chocolate arm coiled in the window. From
blind trees, steam whistles. Wheels grow
noise on rails. The burly black
locomotive barrels into the straight, builds big, slow

breathing hard brakes by, jerking
a hundred hoppers. Thunder follows
fading with the caboose; withdraws.
Quiet sucks in as sky sharpens, hollows.

The sunball bronzes, sinks. Heat
blurs thinner. Scattered cars
pick at the crossing now. The street
goes gray. The sky is washed, ready for stars.

*[12]*

## ARRANGEMENT IN NATURE

One stands, deep buckled into stones, who grudge
way, down into dark ground. Deep scored, brown
bole and waist buttress formality
of branch bent to salute coils swarming with sightless years
lost. Still in strength lurks somewhere
a curve here, there a shy bend of adolescence deprecates
but is absorbed in these mature manners. So stands he

and all eyes are all elsewhere. Circling the site
round hills recede, clouds turn improbable in blue
and distract, but elsewhere still again
curtseys willow grace, or nubile aspens, shy
but seeming ever within reach, beckon
to absolutely impossible communions; or nearer in April toss
the heads in flowers of apples, pretty confusion now
before pink grays (as belle fades all too fast
to fabulous beauty, past days dimmed in dowager);
as bushes whisper, and stir of green intimates
that all about
are false consents to marry, tremulous yes on every side
(and tendrils all golden to finger, see!).

But Two stands, half opposite, not unaware
of the courtesy in acknowledgment, male
to maiden and melting green. No warm in stare
here; irony guards tenderness: shoulder
modeled to half experience turns half away.
Gesture says nay.

There is no future. Yes, but deep
under, pushing, months are inch, below
cold stones, roots grope blind, know

[13]

block and deliberately recoil, then slow
push, past dirt bagged in water, bones
trickling, and grow
fingers: and nothing more, no seed here, no
mouth: it is not marriage, no.
Yet here, deep, past block
of boulder, buried mole, blind and slow
shall hard fingers interlock?

[14]

# ROMANTIC LANDSCAPE WITH STORY

Drenched in wet silver, pale with olive and still
with flowers upon the folded hands of day
the garden at the bottom of the hill

sleeps in arrested expectation. Mail
dramatic on the outline of the rock
a black knight rides his armor down the trail

in quest of histories lived long ago.
Where are our amoureuses? Are they all gone?
But in the lyric valley, dreams below,

memory burns the banners of old nights;
the chimes of stars turn pale upon the hour;
and there, as gardens dawn, and as the lights

of twelve day-candles wink out one by one,
my love walks tenderly where cherubim
choir their rosalbas in the silver sun.

*[15]*

## DESPAIR IN SEASCAPE

Here is the fix: an hour of time crossed over
a mile of beach to hold disparate
materials, as dunes, boats,
assorted anatomies and almost any amount
of water.

      One end of a mile
anchors on those swings, pinwheels, and bannisters a mile
makes into toys; one end smudges off
into soft strokes, haze of dunes and undefined
limit of surf. On feet shoveling
the dry loose hills, on feet (the same) paddles
to smack the wet hard flat
of the afterwave, traverse, loop in, and hold
the scenes of which this mile is composite
in the sightless frame of an hour.

                 Or try.

                   Because
any here is elsewhere before you can pin
it to when; because the breaking, the broken, and to-break
wave sucks into itself and wipes
its shine off the sand before the sand
is through shining; because the child's
sea wall, slapped on as slime, is cement, is sand, is wet
no-shape and no wall; so because
on this material symmetry all moves
except the color of the sand, all sounds
except the silence of the dunes.

*[16]*

                    Or no? Because
seen gull, shell, leg, spade, chair
escape through holes in that gray envelope of nerve
we pull around them, will not stand and be
anything simple like dimensions?

                    The child
spading his bucket is that child you thought you knew
how to reshape and hang upon the mind,
and collapses without weight.


                    Far out, an arc
of marlin, jumping, hanging, clubbed like exclama-
tion points could never be believed
before gone and turned by memory into birds, about
whom nothing is improbable.

                    Even
a detail of nuns walking against the foam and gray
of breakers seems to fly like fragments
of those bird thoughts that haunt the changes of the sea.

All the most loved and vulgar knees and knobs,
angles of people, posts and piles, also specials
as marlin, nuns, blimps, storms
became as wingless, slipping in fragmentary space,
more gone when they were there than they are now.

Dufy, Grandma, or Alice should have painted
this poem I could not write.

*[17]*

## SONNETS FROM THE ENCYCLOPAEDIA BRITANNICA
### FIRST SERIES

*Omsk*

Stands in the middle of a treeless plain.
In January, winds pile snow; in May,
sand. From the Ob by steamer, and by train
from Vladivostok, or by pony sleigh
from anywhere, it is accessible.
The streets are made of mud, the houses wood
(stone under construction). Educational
societies flourish. Industries include
the making of machinery and beer,
foodstuffs. And when, in 1917,
the army of the Bolsheviks drew near,
the town was full of western refugees,
who fled on east, and strewed the way between
with dead from cold, fear, hunger, and disease.

*Ona*

An Indian tribe, once in the interior
of Tierra del Fuego; giants, or akin
to giants; great hunters, and men of war.
Their chief food was the meat, their dress the skin
of the guanaco. Seldom did they sleep
in houses. They used hides to break the cold
out of the wind. They were concerned to keep
the Ona young subordinate to the old
by making tribal candidates go through
a rite of masks to learn theology,
then live alone two years, and so grow stout
and confident. They feared devils and knew
one supreme spirit. Ona mythology
is very rich. The tribe has now died out.

[18]

*Onagraceae*

A family of dicotyledon.
In Britain, the small herb Ludvigia
grows in damp pools, but in America
it is false loosestrife. Pollination
chiefly by bees and lepidoptera,
or when the flowers are pale and open on
the evening, as in evening primrose, one
may use nightflying insects. Clarkia
with epilobium hirsutum, known
as the great hairy willowherb, are still
to add. The flowers are regular in shape.
The New World breeds them in its temperate zone,
but tame oenothera biennis will
grow wild in Britain as a garden escape.


*Hara-kiri*

There are two kinds, compulsory and free.
A gracious note comes from the emperor;
with it a dagger. Friends and family
kneel in a formal circle on the floor.
Beside you kneels your second (Kaishaku).
You confess, are handed the dagger. This you put
below the waist, drive home, and draw it through
the stomach, ending with an upward cut,
while the Kaishaku swings his sword upon
your neck. This is the old, forced way, not now
performed. The other kind is often done
even today, but the book does not say how.
I gather that you are allowed to do
it your way, so long as the knife is pulled clear through.

*[19]*

SONNETS FROM THE ENCYCLOPAEDIA BRITANNICA
   SECOND SERIES
*(N.B. All information is derived from the edition of 1936)*


*Hirohito*

Now reigning emperor of Japan, and son
of Emperor Taisho. He was visiting
in Europe when, in 1921,
Taisho retired from public life, leaving
his son established in the regency
for the next five years or a little more
(for this regime, see JAPAN: History).
Then Hirohito became emperor.
The new reign was officially designated
the period of Showa (Light and Peace),
and the Mikado blessed this period
with his own manifesto, circulated
through all the realm, and laying emphasis
on harmony at home and peace abroad.

*[20]*

## Hiroshima

Fortunate in its lovely situation
beside the waters of the Inland Sea,
Hiroshima has raised its population
from about a hundred thousand (1903)
to a quarter of a million souls today.
The city stands on a small plain, between
hills and the islands scattered on the bay.
Its fame is partly due to the serene
and nearby presence of divine Bentin
on her small island, and to the belief
that she bestows an influence from heaven,
for she is god of radiance, and has been
adored by pilgrims, constantly.

                       The chief
temple dates from the year 587.


## Hitler

Bavarian politician, Austrian
by birth. Once draughtsman, later editor.
His first putsch failed, but later he began
the N-S party. Versailles and the War
had left Germany sullen and embarrassed
by debts. So Hitler was successively
chancellor, dictator, führer, and at last
Reichs-Führer with supreme authority.
He has been violent against the Jews,
is charged with excesses in party strife,
has re-armed Germany and suppressed free news.
Hitler is said to lead a private life
both simple and sincere. He does not use
tobacco or liquor, and he has no wife.

# MEMOIR SUGGESTED BY RECENT REVIVALS: F.S.F.

One is to remember the way fragments of a rose
disintegrate to minor fragments when pressed in
a memory book
and how the identical and breathing rose would look
fastened against a twenty-year-old midnight with a formal pin.

One is to dim his eyes on photographs and read
them while the foxtrot toils on the victrola, scan
the personal poise
of little girls in dancing-school hair-ribbons, boys
in norfolk jackets. All look slightly boiled, but are admired American

specimens dehydrated from our ardent youth.
The brittle music opens and the night is kind,
as a live flower
intimately unrobing in a petal shower
strews all in white the chopping waters of the mind;

and May was miracle when all were wild and young,
and it is Mediterranean whose small tide-heaves
sea-comb the drifting hair
in summer glints of drowning Vega and Altair;
and it is northern autumn borrowed in a fall of oaken leaves.

The manikins. Were they stuffed dolls manipulated
by remote control to posture in the pose
of flesh and blood,
or is there fragrance in the air where these have stood?
I cannot judge between the book-pressed and the severed garden rose.

[22]

## VOYAGE OF DISCOVERY: 1935

Shall we go on with it? Driving ever seaward?
Invisible wings outride this narrow passage.
We see towers golden on the sand. We hear sirens.

The foam flanks widen, the world is split obliquely
after the wind and wings have blessed the burden
of oars swept to the hammer beat no longer,

after the sails were scrapped and the trefoil blades
grind vaster trembling hulls forever forward,
after these and after, the same way always;

the water wrenched astern is a net of wishes,
epitaphs of next years, and the way ahead
tomorrows meeting mortality, imaged islands,

and left and right tomorrows that never happen,
and if you swing the helm and the rudder answers,
sleeve by arm they follow, and still are sidewise.

Maybe the yellow horns quiet the grave water
at Cherbourg, the Solent trodden circumspectly
by giants, the armor and huddle of spears, Manhattan,

San Salvador or Vineland, the northern break
of continent with ice, it hardly will matter.
It will have been a false hope. It will have been

barely the other side of the wings outriding.
They are there, the lovely abstractions, the ifs and maybes,
the forever beyond, the fixed and fugitive,

[23]

the not anywhere, the always elsewhere islands.
Shall we go on with it? Driving ever seaward,
the spoke turning and the next spoke turning with it?

A people's purpose is to build its own death,
to be impatient of its youth and remember
that youth completed as a bright grief lost to it,

and break its heart to be young again, and be older,
and build that age in bridges and guns and armor
and meet its death by turning over tomorrow.

It is useless and there is nothing else to do.
The way to recapture is to go ever onward.
It is the only way left though you die of it.

O ever sheathing and seeming always forward
drowned seeming in blue dimension and lost water,
the rocks seaward, the templed capes, the green shallows,

the bright slopes hillward; in your lakes the swans
as by the strand your ships lie ever quiet.
We came there never but remember dying.

[24]

# EQUATIONS ON A TRIAD

These three,
Faith, Hope, Charity,
if Hope is Hope and future is despair
in hope, and Faith is myth and memory,
if Charity is love and love is care,
these three,
memory
act and morality
are mirror, kiss, infinity.

Immediately there is a field where green is ripped
to thunderpulse in the bladefooted gallop of three
white horses. There is a green tree stripped
to the white heart, with iron in her side.
There is a small beach edged in April sea,
and three tall girls
with hair rinsed in the wind and naked eyes
walk down it one by one
as pale sun drifts the blondeur of their curls:

since memory is a dance caught at the ocean side
and hope a wounded tree
and love is a green field where horses run.

Or through the strings of brain and brain of sense
comb out, and purge,
and fish for innocent fingers; so submerge
the lucency of act; so alter tense,

let memory live idea again and what has been
be index of the still unseen
where, as the callous horns the hand of innocence
the wound beneath is green.

[25]

Those were a morality of nature; these
are keys (can be my keys)
to read my text or pencil out in minor scope
three syntheses
in understanding: Myth, Love, the idiot Hope,
in the grandeur of syntax or the continent scale
of grammar, past present conditional,
love substantive and adjectival past,
and future hope at last
the deadly process of material.

## NEW HOMES

Here where la belle lay dreamy in the bois
dormant, carved in the slumbers of a thousand years,
the figures of our sleepless nights invade
under green choirs spring's sleeping incunabula.
So the barbarian beast now paws and tears,

gobbles and chews green splendors and gray boles
through gouge of ground, scooped underbrush, and murdered trees.
So the dark memory of the wood is made
a dream of brick to house a thousand souls
in parcels of split-level domesticities.

Where are the slopes that leafed and shaded young delights,
where is the sorrel, and the ferns where lost we stood,
the footpath through the bracken where we stopped and played,
except where still, disturbing wiser nights,
the angers of the forest mutter in our blood?

# NIGHT SHIFTS

From twelve to two the locomotives in
the yard were busy with noise, crumbled the dark
distance with motions of their rituals,
slammed, coupled, shunted, switched, unhooked, returned
to lines of boxcars dark and docile waiting,
and slammed and coupled.

                              In the miles of night
the brain, his base half under sleep, half bare
in the dry spells of the clock and the gray time,
rode in their iron music, sat the grooves
of benches, stared at posters, counted digits
of time tables, and through the dirty panes
heard the night dragons coughing in their sleep.

Who is this sideman who strides through the gray
pulling me on a string, whose purpose wheels
my feet down years of rails and winter streets,
who builds my brains with cities never seen,
for whom I am a rag, a sponge to squeeze
for drops of lyric image, at whose slant
I am a paper in the wind,

                        and in
whose night, when the rain dries, the locomotives
bang their iron sonatas on no sleep?
Half white half gray, sunk to the neck in slumbers,
the bare mind dries in the wind as rain
has dried on stone and leaf, and down the miles
of winter dark my sideman slams and hooks,
shunts and uncouples dark and docile boxcars
all the gray times between, from twelve to two.

[27]

## THE FREIGHTERS

We watched the freighters and their classic brows opposed
to ocean on the pale Saint Lawrence waterway
solemnly crease, unsmoothe, and harrow the blue calms
and ride their masts to where the hulls squared slowly,
loomed through the gray
sails at the skin of the sightline, and were gone.

How far, we thought, between the continental slabs,
shall these calm edges stick and twist in the gray
tempers and the slub of the foamy stuff, each
caught as a kestrel fights the air with mere
strength to stay
the world below his struggle of wind and wing.

With such thoughts—no more than an antique legend of men drowned
in the gloom of memory—we outraged the v-shape and the cool wake that
    pulls
the swan's progress of slow freighters riding
their masts in spells of silence to the edge of sight
past where the hulls
grew square and big among the gray sails, and were gone.

[28]

DRY LIGHT FROM PYLOS

〒' ᄂ⊕‡ 日    ⋀≡ᄈ  የ⋔=ᄈ  የⅩ'-ᄈ  ㅌ⎸

1

They come scratched on small clay slabs, from immemorial
stony places; contain obvious numerals; signs
for commodities, things, persons; and syllable
marks, now solved. They run to very few lines.

The fond eye can see a pitchfork, brush, or rake,
a handled basket or an anchored heart,
a butterfly, a four-candled birthday cake,
or proper heroics, chariot, throne, axe, dart.

What is in fact the woman-sign may become
to the imaginative, a close-girt
Minoan lady with enforced bosom.
The man-sign, much like, has crossed legs, no skirt.

But these are ideograms. The syllabary
offers for *pu* a graceful animal,
while *da, ro, pa,* and *to* among them vary
the patterns of the cross; and almost all

make language now, deciphered to a kind
of Greek. Contents: sheer fact; inventory,
lists, and accounts of work. You will not find
heroic action, myths, or poetry.

2

Reading from left to right, the row begins
with a five-syllable word which seems to spell
*a-ra-ka-te-ja:* spinner, one who spins?
The woman-sign follows, with a numeral

[29]

tally, thirty-seven. Then the basket, then
a square tripod; so, *ko-wa;* it will mean
girls. There are twenty-six. Then *ko* again
with a different tripod. *Ko-wo.* Boys. Sixteen.

Last stands a sign, a sort of debased C.
It means some kind of measure, used for food,
grain, drink, or total diet, which will be
something quite basic, and not specially good.

Thirty-seven workers with their woman-sign
and fatherless girls and boys on patient feet
stand there forever waiting in a line
for whatever they are to be given to eat.

*[30]*

# WAITING FOR THE BARBARIANS

*From the Greek of Constantine Cavafy
(Konstantinos Kabaphes, 1863–1933)*

Why are we all assembled and waiting in the market place?

It is the barbarians; they will be here today.

Why is there nothing being done in the senate house?
Why are the senators in session but are not passing laws?

Because the barbarians are coming today.
Why should the senators make laws any more?
The barbarians will make the laws when they get here.

Why has our emperor got up so early
and sits there at the biggest gate of the city
high on his throne, in state, and with his crown on?

Because the barbarians are coming today
and the emperor is waiting to receive them
and their general. And he has even made ready
a parchment to present them, and thereon
he has written many names and many titles.

Why have our two consuls and our praetors
come out today in their red embroidered togas?
Why have they put on their bracelets with all those amethysts
and rings shining with the glitter of emeralds?
Why will they carry their precious staves today
which are decorated with figures of gold and silver?

Because the barbarians are coming today
and things like that impress the barbarians.

[31]

Why do our good orators not put in any appearance
and make public speeches and do what they generally do?

Because the barbarians are coming today
and they get bored with eloquent public speeches.

Why is everybody beginning to be so uneasy?
Why so disordered? (See how grave all the faces
have become!) Why do the streets and squares empty so quickly,
and they are all anxiously going home to their houses?

Because it is night, and the barbarians have not got here,
and some people have come in from the frontier
and say that there aren't any more barbarians.

What are we going to do now without the barbarians?
In a way, those people, they were a solution.

*[32]*

# LOUTSA BEACH

Here, where the pillion riders with their bucks
sprawl in the pineshade, and the oleanders grow
red on the ruins of a house, and boys in trucks
ride from the factories to swarm the beach below,
the Nazis' squat pillbox
desperately defends the coast from nothing at all
but wind and water piling blue on the sea wall.

What thins the sun upon our backs is here
and with us, and we brought it with us, and assume
the shadow like a towel across our shoulders, peer
backward in haste. The giant slept in the next room
last night. This is the fear
that dried upon the wind after the Persian bones
were shucked in holes and sunken under tons of stones.

July and banners of the blown coast wheel
stormily up to dare the northeast and the night
dimmed in the cities of our brain, burst in a peal
of brass and bravery. But what makes the wind so bright
is still that thin, that real
terror that turned the Germans green and made them break
a house apart to guard what no one wished to take.

*[33]*

# THE WINTER STORY

Now on his bare bright pole, and wheeled with ice,
our balanced blue and brown and white partitioned ball
spins out of time
complete into time born, as in a winter stall
between the animals a new child cries
waked here at midnight on the chime.

And beat of angels' wings, slow and immense,
ponderously disturbs the far-dropped atmosphere
where space is blue,
and lonely kings from their cold towers assemble here
with shepherds out of stony fields, with citizens
in furred gowns, and with me and you.

Airwalk of angels, riding kings, and people,
shepherds, with bearded burghers and bland servants, come
to Bethlehem
as the world's music rings her children home
in chains of bell-notes breaking from the steeple
on us, where we may kneel with them.

*[34]*

# ANTIPHONAL

We have made the stone speak, featured the clay.
We have sculptured in gilt close curls over the ears
to carve ever a mask, ever a moving silence,
in even the inked word and the brain's web limning
a sign, graph, idea;
as who handle water's weight, basket the wind
(in the songs, in stone, paint moves over the paint)
deflect elsewhere the model, other the throat surrendered,
and turning the live flesh on the eyes' screen, mirror
a doll there, a dream.

We can mark the words' sound, ear to the beat
of the lips in their speech bent, pore over the scrolls;
we watch and admire, give you our eyes and voices,
and know the design spun is immense and important;
we hear, hush, obey;
but the meaning drowns in sense, eyes into eyes.
For your wounds we have pity, hands, water and oil
adoring the deed, caught with the riding splendor
and using the male force to our own need measuring
propound there delight.

Koré is Persephone and the moon really
is Artemis and Koré, Ashtaroth is Rapunzel
blanched in the milky moon, princess in the window
leaning on white elbows is also Koré
and Danaë drowning in gold is
Koré and Persephone, and they knew properly
ritual and figure, smile in wood and they danced to it:
symbol that means nothing, girl in the cornfield
standing in gold tassels whom once we waved to
and kissed her and knew in August.

[35]

Logic is abstraction and it is the stuff really
informing the need for action, action is the mind wearing
substance to stir substance. Accidents are female,
death, sex, and hunger. But your own hot god is
the sunflare on whom actual girls are
incident. We know it, adore you properly,
paraphrase and statue, eyes in stone and they painted them,
figure that is all meaning, man at the stars' edge
leaning beyond mystery that once touched us
and lived, through us, idea.

We would have known really and forever
(if we could have stayed, if we could have stayed)
Rapunzel to make you and the idea
burn single down the calendar, if
there had been no wars
and no argument.
We wear across our throats the flower and the picture.

We understand really and admiring
(if you had waited, if you had waited)
accept and yield in the shadow of ideas
one thing meaning what you wish, if
we may keep our moon
and our mysteries
and be (time into time) your image and memory.

[36]

# EPIGRAPHICAL NOTE

They arranged what was left and put it away.
Lysidice was young enough to lie alone.
Her house and the bones of her house were there to stay.
We read, from the incised stone:

*I tell those who come here: there shall be a curse*
*on him who shall handle, dirty, or defile*
*me and my image, or dislocate, or force,*
*or shatter, obliterate, remove anything. May God not smile*

*on him, but smite him with terror of the eyes, distress*
*his wits and body with fever chills itch blight;*
*may he not tread ground nor sail water; die childless;*
*go cold in the sun and blind in daylight.*

And so forth. Lysidice died and meant to stay dead.
She had stood in the sun. She had loved poetry
and truth, as surely as she was sweet and young, she said.
She did not want to die. Now let her be.

They excavated, intensely loving, collected
the fragments, read her, and sorted her in a sieve.
She is now scientifically resurrected,
and these bones live.

[37]

# MONUMENTAL

In Schönbrunn stands a hunk of statuary.
Slabs of old armor no one ever wore
in any age, dog-Greek-cum-Latin, vary
the martial attitude around a core
of marble nonsense. So they stuff with blanks
the shirts of Mars. Does opposite Venus drape
a featureless anatomy, and thanks
to new look mitigate her lack of shape?
So obvious my myth. Not brawn of shoulder
as never bulging bust, not even bone
and garbage once humanity can moulder
in this preposterous pinnacle of stone.
Nor Mars incarnate nor his Cytherea
can populate a petrified idea.

*[38]*

## RISE AND SHINE

At the big trumpet we must all put on
our dentures, tie old strings to knees, adjust
shank upon socket, wig to cranium, bust
on ribbed architrave, fastidiously don
our properties, and blink to face the sun.
Farewell, dream-image cankered in our dust
and sweets shrunk in the brain, farewell, we trust.
Uprise, o fragment brethren. We have won,
for, halleluia, these dry graves are torn.
Thin bugles crash the valley of our bones
to rock the vultures wide away and scare
the griffin from his precipice; as, worn
and damp, we crawl like grubs from under stones
to scarf our loves in paradisial air.

[39]

## THE BRINK

They said: When we came into those seas, the mast peak
shot leaves; the wood grew, groaning; the air was
sticky with grapes. That musing iron beak
bit seas no longer, but like a scythe in grass

was hushed. About then world's end was our lee shore.
And we believe, when stack and siren bloom,
and doubled left and right these wake-wings flower
astern into perdition and the gloom

on the world's eyes. Vines strangle every spar.
The oars broke into serpents in our hands.
We knew those islands, and the end not far.
And now the captain's eyes are bronze, a man's

feet petrify. The wood weeps. Silver and glass
branch into rose and shoulder; willows weave,
are arms. Below, the water turns to grass.
Beyond, those island bells. And we believe.

*[40]*

# INVICTUS

If we can only go on saying what we must go on
saying; if our voice is mournful monotony, as rain insists
all dripping night; if we protest too much the malevolence

of our dirty-gray intentions and our morning-afters of lovemaking,
we are not necessarily waste or weary; we may still be
the bat boy who made the team, the third son who was stupid.

We have passed the dry tree and said goodbye to the thorn on the rock.
We waded the smashed green thunder of the river that forbids
hope forever. We have not found the white poplar nor the water

of memory, but we are still walking. While ant lugs
home the twenty times his size slain bug, while dung beetle
wrestles his intolerable Atlas ball, while son

of a gun of a spider climbs up the water spout in the rain's face,
bless our heroics, please. I said we passed, then lost, certain landmarks
in the shouldering dark; the white rock, the orange tree, and the voices,

and we are still walking where we must walk and because we must go
on walking, and having passed much more than this we have forgiven
and thrown away the bitterthin of selbstmord longed for through rain.

A smashed toy or eyes given elsewhere made us passionate
for water of oblivion once, but we crossed over Lethe
and started up the other side of the valley. The rockline escapes

backward as we climb, and what is beyond eludes, invisible
always behind a slowly reeling wall. But is there (we knew this
bathing by bare rock half inside the cold mountain)

*[41]*

and is a thing in itself, positive, peremptory,
not in the shadow of a borrowed grace, not to be endured
for the sake of something else. Nor cross called us,

nor moon's obelisk, snake, moth-urn of dead spirits, bull god
drowned god hanged god. Nothing. No god. But inside
the furious anatomy we fought, with a sword that could not

imaginably cut anything, the invasion of shadows. We passed
the sad tree, and the rock, the well of indifference, the night shaken
by the wings of bats, and in desolate morning cross over and climb to

a shelf-rock half way up the other side of the valley.

*[42]*

# HERCULES AT THE CROSSROADS

Through drenched grass, dawn unmisting, the April day's
prime hour, to a place where a spring comes cold in the shadow of poplar
    trees
and the cross-arms of the pounded road branch, two ways,
young Hercules
trudged, singing the morning up. And there in the shade
two girls waited him. She of the left-hand fork stood pale
and sweet, in a flowered dress, and smiled with made
lips, and allured him with a blue gaze, and sidled forward to hail

her hero. "Hercules. Here your way lies, my way. Here.
Take my hand, I will show you, but see how temperate, gentle and green
it goes. So shall your dearest life go with your hand in mine. Never fear,
I shall not leave you. Between
here and your days' end think nothing but cool progress, soft-soled
walking, sleep for hours, blithe company, agemates outwrestled, girls—yes,
    creamy legs, blond
looks; long nights of shorn white rosefall; for sedate age, goods and gold;
green sinews, honors lightly lifted, good memories. Look not beyond.

This is real." She ended, down-lashed, demure. And presently now, she
of the right-hand way came forward, queenly and sober, and by no means
repellent with her dusky plaits and grave eyes, and told him: "See
where your way leans
to the rock-base and the skinny thorn, the dry of the gorge where crickets
buzz through bones in bare sun and the big animals move in the night.
Haul up the stony grades day by day and scratch for sleep in the thickets.
Dry bread, strong food, scant water. Furthermore, you will have to fight

the hazards that fester our ways. The coarse footpad, ruffian, grifter, wizard
    and phony
shall test your nerve and brain, gristle and grip. Your pace will be slow,
your nights dogged and bare, days thin, and the trail stony.

[43]

I shall not go
with you. You are alone. Good luck and good bye." Hercules
stood footlocked and black with doubt, brow bent;
then chose, turned right, and stepped out of the poplar trees.
His eye slid once to the left. He waved and went.

Now here began a succession of sick and disastrous years
for the tough, the greedy, the cruel and sly of the world, here began
a most pitiable outcry, thumping and struggle as he laid them all by the ears.
The strenuous little man
who fought from grinning helm with spear or bare with his bones, club,
        wrenched broad boles,
mashed snake heads, speared pounded butted or strangled lion and bull,
outsize pig, giant and ogre, and the monsters crawled away and hid in their
        holes.
Much done. But a thin and ragged life. Who has told how scarred and
        twisted, how pitiful

and used, the hero who walked the grand peaks in the end of his time?
A sad strong man, remembering every fight
and harsh from sour triumphs, fear and sickness, the gift of his prime,
the bare night
alone in the slum of the mind, the inward niggle of doubt.
Had he chosen right at the fork of the ways? Was it worth
the beating it took to pacify and set right a world torn inside out,
and fight his way to being the best man on earth?

This is a moral and momentous story I tell.
Here is the Y-shape of tragic choice, Hecate's fork, our sprung three-piece
        cross;
the trails to heaven and hell.
Yes, but which is which? The philosopher's gloss
I give you is one way of the fable, for the refined spirits
to read and ponder. Crasser souls will have it that Hercules
never was lonely. He was a cram-eater, a lap-handling bully boy. Doubtless
        with merits
but much rewarded. We disagree. Now back to my scene at the trees.

The dark girl had told him nothing whatever about any reward.

It is true, he is chapeled with St. Demetrius and St. George, a hero in glory
with angelic sword. .

He is said also to have loved many lovelies along the way, but this will not
accord with our story.

The somber she of the right was gone from his life.

But brute work captures charms and heroes sometimes land in the lush. Did
he ever see his little friend

in the flowered skirt again? Find her waiting after all at a last crossroad and
make her his wife?

I do not know. But it seems established Hercules married well at the fiction's
end.

[45]

TUDOR PORTRAIT


Brusque shoulders and bluff beard,
hated, caressed, and feared,
hornbeam-and-hickory-hard,
gartered and starred,

in slash and puff complete
he stands, all male six feet
and fourteen stone of him,
bulky and trim

astride the austere hall,
big brute divinity,
to master from his wall
Christ Church and Trinity.

Saint, devil, ape, or man?
Soul perfect shaped or maimed?
Human or God's the plan
that left him (named

Defender of the Faith)
to win at point of death
his bitter and his brief
uncouth belief?

Manwolf loose on the land,
reformer with red hand,
verse maker, lout with Latin,
savage in satin;

[46]

coarse hulk of glory stopped
on the last bed of all beds
in a dream circle of lopped
and leering heads

from gross and glittering past,
saw he yet at the last
through the brain's breaking screen
what he had been:

monks' bane, so faith shall flower;
strong king, so kings shall cease;
brute, that there be no war
on earth, but peace?

So judge. But what he saw
shows nothing in jowled jaw
where, stiff astride the wall
of the harsh hall

he built, gaudy and grand
in sceptre, star, and crown,
on strong new worlds he planned
the king looks down.

*[47]*

## BARBARA

*(Young Jemmy Grove on his deathbed lay)*

If I am to be judged and sit apart
in scarlet shame
to wear the favors of my lovely name
upon an iron heart,
I do not know
what I was meant to be
nor why I go
as cruel Barbara, rung home and led
by bells to my cold bed;

since, though I drag my depths for some drowned, dim,
and perished thought
lit with the smiles and eyes they think I ought
to have surrendered him,
I find no love
I was supposed to know
for Jemmy Grove,
nor why his love for me should make me say
that I shall die today

for my true love for his true love that died
on a sick bed
for me, Barbara, cursed with rhymes and led
by bells, in scarlet pride,
to lie alone
without the power to change
on my gravestone
the legend of the lies that shall be said
of me when I am dead.

[48]

# THE WOUNDED

*"The Bomb is the Biggest Thing in our Life"*
*"Nous sommes trahis"*

### 1

A ball of dishonor swims in the dark of moons.
We are a corporation of treasonable dust, and our dust
nurses death by fire in the pit of her own loins.
O Aristotle, flower lives, ape moves, but man is reasonable.
Therefore we are betrayed;
and what is decay in my bones, tetanus in my heal, copperhead in my path,
    but this
which is silver in singing and witty grace of iron in speech
and a ceremony of stars in the mind's cold contemplation;
which is formal sweetness of calculus and grammar?
What that is not lovely
brought us to this shame, ulcered our heel, pounded the powder
of our probable holocaust and terminal Bikini?
And where, if a hand shall lift us
at last from the foaming pit and we win the islands,
shall that be found which shall incorporate our salvation,
if not small, folded, writhing
deep hearted in the ulcer?

[49]

## 2

Oh his rock, Philoctetes,
poking the scum at the beach break,
a crippled crow of a man, watched wings
circle expectant
of meat, flesh of my flesh crawling on the bones' weariness.
Contemplating his foot,
Philoctetes, myth man and symbol,
thus to self: My blue mirror,
pale platter of argent and azure,
scurf-rimmed to the bend of dirt and dishonor,
swarms under slime the glitter of fish, green hair of the mermaid
undine idea sublucent.
Haze lipping the hard horizon
hoods large lovely men who must choke on large notions:
a fort to burn, a pretty prince to shoot down.
They have dust to lick, knees to double before all this is ended.
No, this smelly bulk is not crow's meat, no rag of feathers.
Look at yourself, Philoctetes.
Wrong stains the heart of nobility:
is answered:
light builds in the wound.
Behold, as the lipped fang-cut reeks in the white foot,
and the huge grace and stateliness of muscle is bitten
to a loop of blubbering pain: yet I cuddle the stock to my cheek
and pick a fall of wings out of the shining circle.
I tell a man to go and he goes. I tell one
to stay and he stays. In the light of a moonlong check and recoil
my corruption is starred in silver.
At the scum of the sea break squatting in the ooze I, Philoctetes,
suck the dry sherds of my honor.

[50]

3

We, who were betrayed
by the angels rinsed in the secrecy of our blood, swept in the loins' liquid,
how shall we tear our crippled meat free from the rock of starvation?
Turn, supplicate the wounded.
Their myth: a sky screaming wings, the gray towers huge in a penitence of
  water.
Their salvation: the mercy of the wrong wind, no moon no glory.
Their character in action: the painted helmets flowers alive in the jungle
  flowers
and a darkness hairy with metaphysical apes.
Turn to Benteen and Reno on the hill swept in the riding terror,
to Mallory and Irvine on the last ledge's escape in a thin sky.
And when the forlorn are as kings among men and the large men are
  forgiven,
and the dagger is a scalpel of mercy,
may the wound sleep at last in the heel; the bomb die.

[51]

## THE BRIDGE AT ARTA

*Freely translated from the Modern Greek (Anonymous)*

There were master masons forty-five
    there by the water's edge,
and sixty apprentices worked with them
    to build the Arta bridge.

All day they would work to build it.
    Each evening it would fall.
Mourned then the master masons
    and their apprentices all:

"Useless the work we waste on this
    and vain the toil of our hands.
All day we strive to build the bridge,
    in the evening nothing stands."

With that there came a little bird
    and across the river flew.
It did not sing the way birds sing
    nor as the swallows do.
When it sang it spoke in a human voice
    and told them what it knew.

"Unless you kill a human soul
    your bridge will never stand,
but you must not kill an orphan child
    nor a stranger in the land.

But there is the master mason's wife,
    and she is sweet as a rose.
Let her come slow, let her come swift,
    to see how your work goes."

The master mason heard him speak
    and death was in what he heard.
He thought upon his little light wife
    and spoke his thought to the bird:

"Late must she rise, late must she dress,
    late must she take her way,
late must she come to the Arta bridge
    to see what we do today."
But the little bird paid him no heed
    but said what it wished to say:

"Rise swift, my dear, dress swift, my dear,
    and swiftly take your way,
and swiftly come to the Arta bridge
    to see what they do today."

They saw her come down the white road.
    They saw the way she took.
The master mason watched her come.
    The heart inside him broke.
From far away she greeted them,
    from close at hand she spoke:

"Good health to you, joy be with you,
    each master and every lad;
but what ails the master mason,
    and why is he so sad?"

"Oh, it is my ring that I have dropped
    inside the foremost pier,
and who will go down and who will stay down
    and fetch it to me here?"

"Now master, I will fetch the ring.
    You shall not be so crossed.
For I will go down and I will stay down
    till I find the ring you lost."

She scarce had gone down to the water side
    and scarce stood in the pier
when "Pull up the rope," she cried to him,
    "pull up the rope, my dear,
for I have searched through all this place,
    and I find nothing here."

Then one threw rubble and one threw lime
    on where she stood below,
but the master mason took a great stone,
    lifted, and let it go.

"Now a curse upon the fate of me
    and mine, for it was hard.
There were three of us who were sisters once
    and the three of us were ill starred.

One sister was killed for the Danube bridge
    and one the Euphrates slew.
Now here beneath the Arta bridge
    I meet my own death too.

Then as the leaves of the walnut tree
    are shaken and drift down,
so let this bridge be shaken, and they
    who cross it tumble and drown."

"Now speak a different curse, my sweet,
    and put the old curse by
or you might curse your only brother
    and he might cross and die."

Then she changed her words, she changed her curse,
    all for her brother's sake
"When the wild mountains tremble
    let this bridge tremble and break.

Let those who cross fall in and drown
    when the wild birds fall from the sky,
for the sake of my brother in a far land
    that he may not cross and die."

[54]

GLAUKOS

Inward your black globe crumbles wearily.
Lean inward past the sinew of the heart.
Far underneath red springs of breathing see
the sober fabrication break apart.

And you have laid aside your yellow hair,
models of motion that were hands are gone
and the free arms and surfaces that wear
tints like a change are dropping one by one.

Stand in the white square of the centre, shed
leaf after leaf the dwellers in your mind
stirred backward whence the green cutwater spread
two ruins wincing down the ways behind.

A debris of bright accidents is laid
about your feet, and in the mediate space
circle your form naked as it was made
and turned toward its own symbol, face to face.

He stands. The prints of shells are in his beard,
the grave arms tasseling green weed that drips
the ooze salt to his feet; the hands are smeared
with pulp; the gray scurf stiffens on his lips.

Yet for your presence light begins to glow
red like a lamp for Mary, and the stone
is shriven of excrescence. Slow and slow
the fragments drop. The figure stands alone.

[55]

The ocean kept him, where Atlantis near
rippled its towers of stone across the gloom
of water falling quiet. He is here.
The sea drains moaning from this shuttered room,

the shells and weed upon the noise, to leave
the stone as live as when the quarry broke
unbosoming his contour. Do not grieve.
Distance was littered in your eyes. You woke

to meet your lover rising from the sea
on the green stairway winding to the sun
between your shadow and your heart. Let be.
Distance has died between, and you are one.

*[56]*

# LEILAH

*From the French of Leconte de Lisle*

Sound of wingbeat, murmur of running springs, have fled
the air. The sun, a cinder, swims across the gay
grass, and with his thief's beak the furtive bengalee
drinks the rich juice of mangoes colored as if they bled
gold. In the king's close, where mulberries ripen red
under bare sky, from which all color has burned away,
Leilah, rosy and languid in the heat of day,
shuts deep-lashed eyes. Branch shade is dark about her head.
Her jewelled forehead leans on one delightful arm.
The amber of her bare foot colors soft and warm
the pearled film of her tiny shoe. She dreams apart,
and smiles upon her dreaming of how lovers meet,
like some fruit grown deep colored, passionate and sweet,
that makes the mouth's desire a lightness in the heart.

[57]

# PANDORA

Two o'clock. The house hums with silence, save
where time ticks in the person of the clock
beside the stair, no more than a dry pulse
held in a vein of amber.

                        Now she comes
alone and barefoot down the stair, and holds
the stopper to the vase she carries. All
that changes through the beating heart of this
midsummer afternoon, goes where her feet
go, and as shadow, over the sunned grass
to where the cool of midnight is forever
trapped in green leaves and tunneled over stones.
She has not looked behind, and now she looks
and sees nothing but summer in the sun,
and takes the stopper from the vase.

                                    Nothing
comes out. She waits, and with her pulse the world
fails in its perfect wheel of stride. What came
out was not seen. It was the time of change,
and not the ripple on the waterskin,
and not the wind that moves the ripple, not
the bent plash where the ripple swims ashore,
but only the three corners of the way
wind is to ripple, ripple is to wind,
and both are to the water's edge, and edge
is merged with wind and ripple in one still
and solemn fact. Who can see fact? She knows
no time of change; but sudden in the blue
a bolt unpins, as in a downward blur
of swallows, what sweet gray imaginings
rinse from the color of behind your eyes
in love's aftersleep. Green foils shudder. Roots
draw in.

[58]

For this, who shall not stand and watch
the beak nod in the rainbow spray of strange
blues, and the smoke of burning houses light
his yesterdays? Who shall not raise from mist
of memory those windows where the film
of pearl is figure? Or who will not leave
his bones to mark the night, and rendezvous
with helm-winged seeds to ride the sky and face
forgiveness in the end of all his days.

Life has begun. This was the act of death.
The penalty of tumult. Here the lines
of shatter in a glass grow big and make
a cloud of fission that will never rain
its life away and die.

        Garden goodbye.

She rises and takes up the empty vase.
The gold of summer is a robe to cowl
her quiet's measure as she tiptoes back
to where the clock, dead sentry, lets her pass,
and where her husband slept in the cool room
and does now know the world where he will wake
is all a world away from where he slept.

*[59]*

# DEMETER IN THE FIELDS

Demeter in the fields walks down the green
slopes, by the grooves of springs and in the grass
of watercourses and the cottonwoods
that cloud and mark the long slant of the valley
on the piled silt of mythic river kings.
This land, spelled in the legends of its names,
dreaming as in a bell of glass at noon,
or closed beneath Orion in the sky
fixed striding, where the daughters of the dove
shine on the bull's black shoulder, and the bear
wheels her bright dipper on the polar star,
this land is hers, who wades in the grain, who turns
the colors of the sloping soil and sees
brown changed to green in May and green to gold
in June.

    This is the goddess of the grain
who by the sea at the horns of rock and by
the time of air burned into day's end, stood
to curse the world with salt, for Death and the Maiden,
for laps of flowers and the young hair so seized
and raped; for her lost daughter in the ground.
But this was marriage and the seeding of years.
The hairy god and his bright virgin keep
the subterranean ritual, and their loins
swarm up in gold and children of the corn,
and on these slopes Demeter of the rocks,
the mother, centered in a trinity,
walks softly as the wings of her folded hands
cradle a blessing on the field of pain.

She is the noon siren sleep. She gives
love under lattices while the clock nods
and blood hums in its drain. She is the sense
of separation and surrender, she
the drowsy sphinx of summer, in whose lens
the serpent and the dove combine to burn.
Her unintelligible magic swims
across the preening eyes of men and girls
adaze along the tawny heaves of fields.

Now in the young time of the year they come
to cut the bronzed and bearded heads of wheat,
stack the lopped manes in golden walls, and blow
the dusty yield of summer into bread,
then homeward, blade on shoulder, hand in hand,
walk slow between the piles of the year's wealth
past the white chapels mounded on the hills
crossed with the arms of Christ, and consecrate
to Mary Panaghia and her saints,
to Isis, Ashtaroth, and the blood of the moon,
to female earth, Demeter in the fields.

*[61]*

# WHITE HARBOR

Slow clouds are bells
in blue drowned
and sleep and die
with cold shells
as underground
wells, and lie
in shattered light
deep blue down.

Walls were white
if walls were,
by golden fringe
on waterblue
sea shawl.
But sands blur
build, winds push
slowly through
ruin, where wall
went.

    Bend back
from water eyes'
asking sweep
and goldenslack
ground lies
in lizard sleep.

Seaward and moored
in jelled blue
the keelboard
dreams true
dreams.

That mound, that not natural hill, heaved, under
piled in drifts of rubbling generations, that earthmound
is it.

Here at the doubled cross, seaward and landward, one arm
of the cross breaking Asia open, one the blue sheer of the Cyprus
main, they built it, or rather not they, or not built, but the moun-
ding started, in dawn utensils being handled, in squatting
by night to the huddle of sociability, in day by day the convergence
of casual ways backfolded on a circle near water and a piling
city begun.

(In night, in the dark of the mother, uncoils
through soft struggle what will be shining, brainflower
that bursts: the manners that make courts, sagacity of the markets:
the little ceremonials of uprise and the bath, food broken
and tasted with others who taste and break food; the small and infinitely
sweet ceremonials of goodnight: and dark: and light: involved
in absolutely ordinary day-things: and dark again, golden
monotony of routine when the world was golden.)

What need pulled the indrift of outlanders on this core
of peoply warmth: and who; it stays uncertain, if only
a serviceable harbor, pale sheet for ships' self-admiration
and land complacent along the sweet bend of the shore. At least
it was not protection, no fat fort to hulk its frown
of military indignation black on its people. This was
entirely a bourgeois proposition. It meant peace.

Islands always meant more than islands: yours
or mine. As on the baked macadam summerhaze
runs ripple of water that is not there, siren allures
seafarer, sand is wells; as memory drowns our days
in stations of the past; as stars of hope
pick out the winter sky that waits, to mark

our pale procession down the western slope
where gone-before-us gibbers in the dark.
Islands are always elsewhere

                              as for
the bleak farmer who weathered a hillside of stones, with his
lawsuits and his calendars of days; his steading
dropped away from the cream and blue, the drenched in danger
and desirable swan's way, gull's way, wheel and plunge of the merchant
ship. At the intersection in midstone, neither blessed with
a shiver of breezes in August blaze, nor sunlight to unsharpen
wounds against winter: lost in the wheels of time worn out
the days of sun, and man and god considerate, lost alike in the fog
of a northern channel sundance of promise to come. In the fixed intersection
of the positively worst time at the absolutely worst place, he sang out
the days of glimmering graces, saw islands but could not name them,
sang out the graces across the slopes of hastening hillsides,
and night revolved in over the scaurs, its color iron
as a grumpy Venus gathered against her sides still golden
attendant cherubs, and trailed them off to simper in sunnier
climates.

        To him, islands immerse in death, and dead men
move magnificent, converse with stately and tall
gestures about nothing in particular, or stride in procession
of brainless grace. Here all men are kings, except that
no men are men.

                But there
          dredge deep down
          in the sand's pile
          gold under lit blue,
          sludge of the Nile
          rinsed clean as bone
          and north dragged
          glims through

where pale lateen
caught the sky's
drench, between
brown arms
and brown eyes,
where days slipped
and laughter bubbled
under starburnt
arch black above
where dim nudes troubled
the waters

(not as in lotus, asphodel, acquamarine
projections of the always-gone, the neverseen
escape of memory through the flights of time-between)

in the mound above
find them, break
the noon sleep,
past block and stone
dig down,
dig deep.

Slowly, and sober with method, pick at first
and spade hack out the holes. Round of a vase
shoulder, or sleeping pot, stir in the torn
earth, and emerge; or half arc of a well;
the angle of a bastion or a drain.
Now the coarse iron checks, and knives suggest
away the mould that clings upon, or fingers
fiddle with, these fragilities.

                    Such mulled
and such disturbed and fragmentary clots
of pattern mean a morning of the world.

[65]

When the last spade has turned, and all the men
gone home; the gold wiped and the splintered clay
glued up; the floors scrubbed bare and labeled, pots
arranged to smile from prim order through glass,
symbols pick out in points of light their years,
and Eden is a fossil in July.

A salve jar is a crucible to make
an ordinary nine o'clock upon
the lips of no extraordinary girl
into a blush, a stammer of amaze
and a wild pulse under bland moons, to hold
as guard against tomorrow and the years
remembered in a mirror.

                    On a dish
chariots and lions, showier, hold the pride
of man's desire, for one in whom no show
was worth the pride and loss.

                              And where they built
their careful and their monumental drains,
smile we at material civic self-importance
that makes their streets and houses other than
sties bleared obscene with dung and slops and flies.
Politic, they guarded skin. No thump of nailed
in bronze Assyrian mace was knotted to
the habit of their hands. (The tissue's schemes
are in their letterclay.) They played it safe
between the looming beetle and the wolf.
A room where secretaries bent might mean
lines of thought twisted into strings, to bind
tissues of fierce desires in sheaves of peace.

This is the suburb, the grocery, the garden
next door. Her stars are ours. Her blood beats to
our pulse.

We own, we sign to and acknowledge
the symbols lying near.
A hoard of golden coins. A pile of swords.

Materially elsewhere, mine in strand
of hair so thinly binding bone on bone, o land
forgotten of your gods, dead in the sand.

Green go they in their brief sun. The broken edges of winter
are iron hooping their horizon's wheel. For the northward water
bitterblue boils, and the hordes stir swarming. Skullfine, arrogant,
limblank; seeing the loveliness shaped in a sword; their blond locks
swept in battlewind; their girls golden, cleanstepping, iceblue
in the long eyes; their babies steeled in cold springs; the destroyers
move.

Green go our people, the sunlight tender about them,
young, not long to live. The bearded hawk of the desert,
the hideous vulture, move and follow. Go gay, my people,
in late afternoon. South of your feet that flitter so lightly
crawl, suspicious with gods, the dark hordes that infect the desert's
thin encounter with trees and the green crescent.

                                                    Fanatics
fidget with knives, they the skilled in despair, the learned
in not, in is ignorant, students of man's diminution
and his honor whittled against the stature of magic and monkeys.

Caught in convergence, gay go

                              (the green lawns shall sear, the
            gracious
and not exceptional houses roar in collapse of drowning
brick; sky glare with gas, and vultures over the playground).

*[67]*

Our world, your world, little world, green go, go gay.

As time drips
the doll's head
jerks.

Then
silence hoods,
gathers, grows
big.

Abrupt on black
crinklecrash thundersplits
forlorn smoking halves.

Nobody even picked up the pieces. Pitiful
and forgotten the splintered city, fluttersmoke
wisping, scattered the track of footbeats vanishing.
They would not tidy their garbage. But no matter.
As reeking midden mounded to buttersoft landscape
and slept, and forgot history, the northmen bent
west from their casual wreckage. Children these
were; meant no harm and had no manners.
They circled back on the strong places, smashed
and rebuilt the beetling citadels; married
their slaves; gracious grew, with just kings
and large liberal populations. The work
of their hands stops our breath. Their speech
strong flex, sweet wisdom, world's wonder.

They, not we. Piled under
drift of time, white harbor
is sand reach by glitterblue of lonely sea.

[68]

The friends were busy elsewhere.
There were not enough swords.
The potential was not there.
Someone wasted the hoards
of gold, or lost them. They fought,
but they could never have won.
The guards were asleep, or bought.
They were done.

Sleep, city,
Let the murderous magnificence pass in Nineveh
howling above your grave; in Egypt hugely serious
over her meaningless mysteries of superstition, serene
contemplation of her narcissus in sacred waters.
Strip stark the splendors, male and female, of Sparta; webswathe
the sheathed and subtle, violet Athens:
Greece, the heartless and haunting in broken glitter of bluesleeved islands.

Sombre Rome outreaches, cramps
you in iron of difficult sinew. Ossifies,
turns rotten in the softer parts.
Saracen bigot and mailed murderous monk
squabble across your grave.

Perhaps you were worth the lot of them: for whom,
at least, a marriage is worth as much as a death:
who love men more than Man:
who would rather have the uninteresting town square rustle on
    Saturday night than have their name written on another part of the
    map.

The whole boiling, rank, incestuous kettle of history throws up
    here and there a radiant splash, which shines and is gone.

Undreamstirred sleep, which is little enough, is left you.
Sleep on, my city.
Sleep.

# THE AUTUMN CLEANING

I tear the past, the lives, the paper brains,
the scripts of scenes, the faces, in a pile
of soiled business, letters too late to answer,
obsolete obligations privately
commingled with an imperfect romance
here, there a blotted grudge, the universe
of paper.

        Photos. Here's a face. The eyes biggen.

Out.

    But two faces more, changed so, so keep.
Be sentimental.

          Old class lists, who were
these people, yes, but I remember you.
The University of Illinois
PhD 1935. Keep that.
This says one hundred fifty-six a month
upon retirement at age 65.
For the steel file. The paper world performs
futures as well as memories.

          Top drawer.
A pipe. A rubber band. A Chinese stamp.
At Pei-tai-ho the decorous donkeys' ears
and bells and trot emerged at Lotus Hills
on the right, and Tiger Rocks, and Black Leg Bay,
rolled in my drumming ear the shell's thunder
caught from last summer's surf, unsealed in blue.

[70]

Now read typed stanzas (if I can!) composed
of headlines and the Battle of Britain. No,
but it was made of boredom and the blanks
of duty time and nothing to do, the cross-
word puzzle solved or stuck, staring at the blue
trousers of the watch officer asleep
on the blond-oak table. Tarry a moment, there
is something else: the editorial gloss.
Praiseworthy technical accomplishment
but find no true emotion dum de dum.
File in the burnbag. Tear the paper brains.

More photographs. How mountains flatten out.
The crash and laughter of a great green wind
down Adirondack slopes. And she. And I.
The cold pool by the rock, the ferns, and heaven.

Maple by slant-crossed mullion and they wait
for me. I live. We'll to the woods again.
The young green heron squatting in his swamp
snapped at the water, wrinkled mercury, spattered
the cathedral hush in a small wet noise.

I tore my past. Brains and blood into ink
is painful transmutation, but when leaves
are torn so, there is pity in it. What lives
in the waste basket now, I shall not know.

[71]

CAPTIVE

*After Theognis*


I gave you wings. Black stone, blue heave shall take
the shadow of your flight. Where men pass, where
legend is live with music, they will make
your name a song, and you will still be there
when all your bones are gathered underground
to sad and private darkness in the sty
of Hades; you shall live still in the sound
of singing. Even dead you shall not die.
For song is mine and I am yours. Then go.
Continents dip behind your heel, appears
Ocean and spinning water miles below.
You ride on wind and a defeat of years.
I made you this. And now you turn from me
as from a child who will not let you be.

*[72]*

# IN THE BEGINNING

There was a first time without anything to remember.
There was a nerve strung in wet shining southward
and the wheels striding over and over
the piston doubled and falling, and the sound
over thinking, and the rails' gleam;
the secret towns, their balance of despair
on caped hills, their tenses of color changing,
Cora, Lanuvium lost to the left, and seaward
the slow green heave of the campagna, screens
about a headlong nothing, a not-yet
folding into an alien dimension
as limestone folds to landscape sealed with blue
of scarfed water and history.

All that time waiting.

But the way back was otherwise, framed
in Campanian yesterdays, and always backward
piled on each other (with your fingers holding
time is lost in the drift). There is another reason
not to throw our nets into the black water
to drag what thin silver of reminiscence.
But if you and I ever need to remember:
our island plunged in rain, and was not there.
The promontories cut cool water level
to yellow bases; the water lifting backward
bared the coast a slant of gray to the drift,
and seaward to the mist Misenum
a fist of peril, and Cumae ever seaward
lit by no mortal sunset. Backward ever

we had the breathing mountain, the earth's anger
buckled under our knees; on the black, sidewise,
crescents of electricity; we had
a mile of sand at Paestum, even before it
a bridge at night between trees . . .

                                If you ever
need to remember, there is one more image
dropped on the shining heap: the mailed knights
asleep in effigy, the vandal sword, the drift
of surprised death, the skeletons of cities,
the strangers with eyes full of sunset and water
unmeasured homeward. There is another leaf
to make once more numberless the leaves
drifted to earth in thirty hundred Octobers,
if we ever need to remember . . .

                                But this is another
time before memory (come, your fingers
on my wrist, myself larger by one person
now, for the way beyond words of your being near me).
We could throw all this away, as we put aside
that island the death of a soul might once have bought
for a moment. We shall not ever need
to remember, any more, there is too much elsewhere.

[74]

## PAST EQUINOX AND UP

Time, now and forever, climb the year and wheel
the hot stars up: burn sun, sluice rain, burst plant, explode
our thunderblush of April and unreel
the winter sleep of animals: hop, crawl toad
and snake wriggle: poison plant close fondle fresh
blooms. Now is the indiscriminate resurrection of the flesh
and shatterfall and pinflash of pain on eyeball and fingerball that feel.

Take it, oh hold it close and close. Outgrows
bigger than ever your brain bulged it in dreams the shape
of the year. This dripping flail of thorns shall end in a rose
to end your roses all, her sprays escape
imagination, all that in cold sleep and the blind
of the year blossomed inside the garden shell of the mind
take, clasp till it cuts and sticks in the wound, tighten and hold it close:

and now: before the brute To-Be, the slow
ox with a fist clumps down the hill and clubs our bones
to dust. Splash once first, struggle. Not for our sweets, no.
Bare shivers the philosopher's anticipation when his stones
are slabs on what has been our fiction. No, but to see
the bruise blacken and wear our personal mark where we
hold, twist, grapple the year before the year goes where we also go.

[75]

## RETURN OF THE IMAGE

What symbol resurrects your spring?

For you were not ever seemingly even in our
intangible past habitation. No echoes ring
your voice. There is not any power

to charm that silhouette of flesh and essence
into more than the contour of ideals.
What symbol resurrects your presence
against a curtain in the mind that feels

only an absence not too large for regret?
It is because of your right and form, too strict
in style of grace ever like ours to be let
drift, a material derelict

populated by ghosts, about those mortal springs
where once your apparition stood
gathered about by afternoon as with wings
of future folding in the maytime wood,

or in the room, with the sun through the glass
dropping light from your wrist against the wall.
Are these things idols behind you? Do they pass
shining behind your life? Does any symbol recall

your transition through another person's shadow
with open eyes and with unfaltering feet?
Will you return, a stranger, to our living meadow
in voice and color complete?

And shall I see your outline on the wall?
Does any symbol recall?

*[76]*

## PROTHALAMIUM

Before we remember this
not yet to be remembered
time, in the time that is,
take these periods ambered

in uncertainty, know
these minutes: edge on bright,
birch on green, gold on snow;
turn your hair in the light,

wrist in water, recall
the not yet, sun in your sleeves
gathered; young winds that fall
to the throat; the lying in leaves;

sand between waves, and between
rocks color, and cold blue
skyward in shallows green
your legs, sun drowning through.

Wind on your throat, recall
the not yet capture and flight
where the shining moments fall
the other side of tonight.

*[77]*

# MIDSUMMER NIGHT

*(Uncle Matthew, why can you not be wholly serious?)*

Silvered in the slow loops of streams and caught
in compass of tamed bliss by countryside
where north goes pale and kind in night and June
to bend gray over green of meadows and wash
the clubbed spinneys to islands on its pallors,
the gothic city pondered (arched and groined
as groves of stone and mediaeval thought,
or Christopher and Queen Anne with domes and courts
bestride the silence of stilled traffic) on her past
told over and over in the bells of her names
(Saint Mary and Saint Peter-in-the-East,
Magdalen, tower and deer park, Oriel
of the Window, Corpus Christi and Tom Quad,
Merton of Duns, and Queens, and Folly Bridge).
Bemused by time's suspension in an orb
calmed by Thule's cream and Hyperborean gray,
the stone-enchanted metaphysician watched
ontology's escape in mullion panes
and moon, and latinists lost Latin. Out
beyond the lights and streets in distant pubs
sounds lapsed, and drinkers dreamed across their beers.

The year at point of turning seemed to hang.

The last train hooted, the last bus wheeled home.

Time gentlemen please.

                The watchman of the dome
clanged out one hundred one.

*[78]*

                    In Long Meadow,
by Witham or on Headington Hill, at Bagley
Wood or dark on Shotover, the clerk
hand in hand with his starveling beauty, the lonesome
undergraduate, the don's daughter,
the strayed tourist and the strayed tourist's wife
caught the reverberations of the hour
and knew love's loss and the glum stride of time.

*[79]*

## TWO OCTOBERS

Circle of gold on gold the year is kind
enough to bind
October on October and the ghost
of a touch lost
between emerges. Take my hand and shut
your eyes; your foot
is deep between Orion and our prime,
your foot prints time,
and the gold month rolls slowly back to green
shining between
slatewater of Nemi and the golden bough,
then and now
forever handfast, and I thought we went
over the bent
hills to Frascati and the pale sweet wine
yours and mine
forever as the forest in between
gold into green
is changed and changed. In yesterday's strong lines
tomorrow shines
unwritten but remembered and lived through.
I thought you knew
how this collapse of spinning color fills
the Alban hills
forever and non-yet, and that it means
all in-betweens
and all our year has gathered up its sleeves
across the leaves.

[80]

## LEGEND FOR A SHIELD

Legend married April and death to breed this
branch of green strength. Trees understand, the rain is
bright accomplice, only our eyes are vexed with
        sun, nor perceive it.

Half your destiny is as gold and amber
luminous. Wear this, and reject that iron
frail with use crossbound to your blazon. Be with
        leopard and gryphon

clear and fierce in mystery, when the skilled lips
bend across your eyes, and you watch the arms' grace
turn and fold, be history, and the charmed eyes
        model your future.

Strike then, innocent and savage, be ware of
April in your star. For a man before you
took the devious way, and his blood remembers
        here, in this poem.

[81]

## AUTUMN EQUINOX

Shoulders in the thin angle of elm the boy watches
his month burn out in maple and sumach, wish drowning
in steep sunfall bannered under the cold skyline.

Reluctant the red lingers, sky-flush west. Red is
the kiss he took to bed last night; the tide beating
wrist to close heart; an answer; a silk dress captured.

This was farewell and love-no-longer. White hesper
and tamarack scratch now punctuate the steel progress
of night's tomorrow climbing up the cold autumn.

*[82]*

# FIVE O'CLOCK

These afternoons of nerve and tissue raise
islands evocative of elsewhere, lost
in the torn gauze of unhistoric days;
lands raw with sunlight, which the retinal ghost

remembers, never having seen; the snow
in feathered mist; the gryphon on the gold;
the slain who walk; the tall black king whose bow
no northern arm could bend. Oh, it was told

myself, and by myself, how on a time
the color of an angel's hair was strung
across my heart. Untrue, untrue. The rhyme
broke out its future when the hand was wrong

who now ropes back his drifted swans to lie
docile as boats in place upon the film
of evening colored water, and not fly
the arrogant sunlight of that young, false realm

where snow and gold and death compact by art
are penance to chastise the winter heart.

*[83]*

# ANNIVERSARY

Where were we in that afternoon? And where
is the high room now, the bed on which you laid your hair,
as bells beat early in the still air?

A two o'clock of sun and shutters. Oh, recall
the chair's angle a strip of shadow on the wall,
the hours we gathered in our hands, and then let fall.

Wrist on wrist we relive memory, shell of moon
on day-sky, two o'clock in lazy June,
and twenty years gone in an afternoon.

*[84]*

# THE SHADOWGRAPHS

Image comes down to live as fact, and turns
in the same motion, and is memory. The process
climbs my long gallery, jogs the score, and burns
in points of color, fancy, and, ah yes,
love. For the same finesse
that changed my copper counters into gold
falters not, sleeps not ever, nor grows old.

What then have I not done, what have I done
with sometimes, not, and never, how to list
my loss against my gain when all are one
and on the vision's glad and deceived mist
the blonde illusionist
performs before my captured audience
her same and golden chores of innocence?

Here is a march of fictions down the road
to nowhere and forever. Did I live
these dolls of faith or die that episode
of fury? Who knows now? Pale, through a sieve
drained days combine to give
substance of what? Who knows? Never goodbye
while the deft hand is sweeter than the eye.

*[85]*

IT

*(For S.L. and A.L., who think of writing)*

Do it, then. If you do,
incontrovertibly know
the worst thing you have done
is the best thing under the sun
if it was written true.
if it was meant to be so.

Never write to please.

A poem is a not-yet.
Then, as you make it, forget
what you imagine to be
the critic who can't read,
the reader who can't see.

Make it alone for you
and yourself.

       Choose
what you mean to do.
But it will be no use.
It will choose you.

You took no life of ease.

Think of the world when you
are in the world. If it will
the world will judge. When you write,
a blind maker, alone
in your individual night,
by steel, be stone.
The world may tear it from you
in its day, when you are through.

[86]

If not, you have made it still.

Despise temperament.
Beyond all else despise
the trick of lineament,
the look of the hair and eyes
the professional veneer,
the Needs of your Career.
Poets as such are dull.
The poem is all.

Live only to understand
only the thing in your hand,
the sight that sticks in your eye,
the wish that sticks in your heart
and will not let you be
until it is made art.

*[87]*

# SESTINA FOR A FAR-OFF SUMMER

SHIP BOTTOM

How gay those bulks that tattered,
years gone, the lace of the blue giant. How gay,
in the Gulf Stream's film of pale calm, scattered
sea monsters at play
off the V of the prow's cool move. Now, shattered,

the giant's toys rot, sanded
and strewn. Oak ribs brown
in air, re-enact on dry water the landed
whale's grin and gasp, as if speared bulks drown
for sky in the lungs and die stranded.

Ship bones commemorate dead huge toys hurled
ashore by angry blue, time
sands their smash. Far out, still, leviathans, swirled
in the swim of transatlantic tides, climb
the arc of the world.

*[88]*

# THE ACADEMIC OVERTURE

Black robes, hoods gold scarlet purple, bright heads
and old beards, the young pacers and the bumbling feet of age
unite now under ceremonial musics, or gaudeamus.

Let us rejoice then in our prime, while how well still
the gown molds the young wrestler's arms, how comely
blonde on black as youth models the robes of learning.

Somewhere about the middle of the procession
I thought, too, how our autumnal heraldries
glow upon the bulks and husks of the elders

to paint a rubric, red and black, on the folios
of forever; while all these stalks strengths flowers
shall be, in some sense, blown heads and florist's litter

swept into bins, and too soon. Or would it be rather
that the dignity, the enactment, the ceremony,
the time in June is eternity established? And through it

unchanged brush the light feet and young voices behind where ponderously
the brasses blare and basses deeply deliver the everlasting
gaudeamus igitur of the elder students.

*[89]*

## MAX SCHMITT IN A SINGLE SCULL

How shall the river learn
its winter look, steel and brown, how shall we
upon our moving mirror here discern
the way light falls on bridge and bare tree
except as in the painting? Cold fires burn

autumn into winter. Here still
the pencilled sculls dip, precise arms beat
the water-circles of their progress. Skill
arrowheads elegance. City Line to 30th Street
is forever, Eakins, your Schuylkill

and ours. What you have done
made us see what we saw. Thus our eyes
after your image catch the steel and brown
of rowers on the water, improvise
by you our colors in the winter sun.

*[90]*

# FEBRUARY LOVES

St. Valentine is gone with his sweet arts
that practice on St. Valentine's day.
How green our winter thoughts incarnate here
in cardboard chocolate and scarlet hearts
where courteous lovers put their loves away
in attics for another year.

Gone, gone the smiles, the pink wings, gone for good
love's cherubs with their silly little
bows. But our season's iconography
displays, a symbol dreaming in our blood,
the virgin of the forest pinned by brittle
glass arrows on a winter tree.

*[91]*

## THE FATHER

*They say the phoenix arrives at the time when*
*his father dies.    Herodotus*


Once a gay wit, subsequently a wretched instructor
with his lilacs and pigeons painted for the Malaga bourgeoisie;
even these painted no longer when the unbelievable son

was thirteen, and the brushes handed to him; the little teacher
relapsed to being Senor Ruiz, father to one who will not
perpetuate the name of Ruiz, but goes as Picasso

after the warm mother he liked. In the new universe
of meager blue harlequins, angled cubes becoming
musicians, bitterly sharpened bulls, and naked

desirable shapes of what age makes for consolation,
where will you find the pigeons or the lilacs, where handle
the brown feathers of such a bird as fathered this phoenix?

[92]


*With full acknowledgement to Janet Flanner's "Profile," Part 1, THE NEW YORKER, March 9,*
*1957.*

# BOOKMAN TO BOOKMEN

To whatever here is done
so do
as if it had been one
by you.

Else leave it to die.
Never
brush a summary eye
over

word lines stuck
in form
round, deep in a book
and warm.

Do not by these know
about,
therefore, also,
no doubt.

Gristle and sinew,
green thews
grow grafted in you;
or lose

in washed lies
all force.
If so, better truly despise
this verse.

*[93]*

# THE LINE

Friends I saw standing in that desolate line.
Final formation. But what used them so?
Outfalls, irregularity, design
or dearth was it that dried their strengths to shells,
or is this only time's iron grace who crowns
his queens and kings, then stacks them out to die?
People like us, and faces that we knew.
It was more than the clock. For I saw too
some green and golden heads among the grays,
and flowers infiltrate the arranged gravestones.
To Armageddon and the game of bones
are guided all formations of our days.

Where faceless prows are ranked upon the tide,
the larvae of the transatlantic fleet
stiffen on those gray waters where they dried:
rats in their brains, and padlocks on their feet.

*[94]*

# HIPPOLYTUS IN MIDDLE LIFE

Stand there, alone and strong,
in your green grove on the hill,
the timeless grass in the meadow.
Think of your sweet unseen
druidess in her green
leaves. Think how still
arm and stride are young.
Fifty feels twenty-eight
and sixty throws no shadow.
Still you have come too late.
The time of year is wrong.

The warm country is here
and we are here, but the time
of the mistaken season
has hung our loves to dry
on the wind, without how or why
or rhyme or reason.

The green barn on the high
line of the hill is only
a row of sticks on the sky
line, ugly and lonely.

Shall we no more to these
woods, no more, where worms
spin their nets in the trees?

*[95]*

Day is a dream of forms
here in whose summer shapes
August color escapes
the hold of eye and sense,
and only memory warms
the thin lines in the brain,
the row of sticks on the sky,
the loves forgotten again,
and who knows why?

Oh, end it, end it. The rhyme
is bad. There is no song
in the thin lines. The time
of the year is wrong.

*[96]*

# THREE GREEK VIRGINS

*1. Seen on Penteli*

In the gray corner, under the line
of the fog, there was a cold
spring, curbed; one contorted pine;
a hut of stones; one old

man bent by the wooden trough;
an icon windowed on a stone post.
The holy angle hoarded its thin forms, enough
to make an emblem crossed

in its own version of what Mary can mean
on mountains, somberly combined above
stone plain and sea: a weather queen
in a cross of wind and one gray shape of love.

[97]

## 2. *Resident by Mistra*

Here on the black butt of the mountain they spattered an angle
of the Morea with their strongholds, so galvanized East to West
in feudalities of stone. How here to disentangle
Villehardouin from Paleologues? That hawk's nest

of a keep tumbled on the crest armored the Frank's baron,
while they below of the thunderous, the now crashed and sunken, lizard-
     written hall
fought him, sword to axe in the bloody defiles, pounded him from his warren.
Saints fade their eastern look on the murals now. South down the mountain
     wall

the Pantanassa crosses her convent in cypresses, serene
strokes on white plaster where nuns are alive next the welter
of wrecked chapels. Beyond, the staggering slopes lean
up into air angels live in, and by St. Barbara's shelter

peoples of the plain ascend in processionals red gold and white
to splash one dawn a year with singing in the cold growth of light.

[98]

*3. Dominant over Mykonos*

Lady of the open and the closed
waters: blessing from the points of your hills the little ships
leashed in the quiet of jetties; as, too, barques tossed
in the straits' fury, blown chips

miserable in storm: Mary of the Sea, who—with attendant Maries
and saints, Elmo and Elias, all who indwell
on the sloping wind those white-candy sanctuaries—
hold as yours this island, breakwater, beacon, harbor bell

and buoy: abstraction of sweet weather: for boats that ride
gray storm as green calm, possessively
throned on cliffs, whose sainted heroes burn at your side:
anassa: despotess of islands: queen of the sea.

*[99]*

# THE GULF STREAM

That day she moved with her smoke, for what wind blew
dallied astern, ripples glassed, stayed with her, and seemed
to mold a sleeping ark, and brown weeds grew
and waved softly in the water; turtles dreamed

supine as scarabs liquidly engemmed
in blue motion, but slow, but slow; the whales
were black gestures miles off, and sharks gravely stemmed
their turns as long green sheaths with arcs of tails.

Fish were not real. Daydream, they seemed to say,
daydream, and gulls were thoughts, and what wings flew
those airs were loves seen lightly, when that day
stopped world and water in one spell of blue.

*[100]*

# AFTER CHRISTMAS

Now, as the stripped tree lying in the corner, the tinsel
globes and stars packed in the box, and the pretty paper
piled at the top of the cellar steps remind us

that the child and shepherds are put to work and the philosophers gone back
where they came from, now morose, too late as usual, let us
reconsider what growths may be coming to bud behind those winter

roses and steels, those cold gray masses that huddle our sunsets.
Yeats and Auden, sages among us, restive and sensitive, flared
their nostrils to some taint of death in the wind blowing

over Bethlehem, and the skies set for our re-enactment
glowed with such a wrong star as to confuse warm disavowal
that the beauty born under the year's heart might be somewhat monstrous.

Can worse than iron be muttering at the thunder-colored
edges of east? Have the peculiar priests, the scholarly murderers
dreamed up some new swallow-all and lemming-drive of destruction?

Let the language of poetry for once square off, try to
face the pragmatical, preposterous pig which Berkeley's
shining tissue of intellect could no more make disappear

than wishing will build us walls for our children. Still, what the world needs
most is philosophy, ever since the mythical magi
saddled from the manger and rode back into the cold desert.

*[101]*

# A THEME FROM THOMAS HOBBES

*Theme and Garden*

If memory is decayed sense, and imagination
is decayed memory, what do you make of you
or what do I make me, seeing I am
what I have seen, mostly?

                        And now decayed.

As, item, in the muddy garden kneels
a woman, nineteenth-century Greek, half draped,
marble, I suppose, and the head knocked off.

                                    Or, item,

the house, eyes (once the windows of sense)
fallen in, the paint on the veranda floor
chipped, and the boards sagging.

                            Item, too, the sofa
in front of the shed faces the street, is horsehair;
double Cupid's bows of hardwood frame the back,
and nobody would sit there in the rain
except with an umbrella or a straw
hat, or as he might pose, with one hand on
his hip, and the other on the broken neck
of the kneeling woman.

                    And the sense decayed
and that was memory, and what was left when memory
decayed too was imagination, and the musty smell
of the garden, which remember is you and I,
is faded sense.

[102]

*Seal Harbor and Marcy*

But how we woke those mornings in the sun
from tumbled sleep and careless strength.

                                          How feet
were fury on the sand and ran the surf,
or found our water, numb blue where it hit
the eyes, but green upon the understones
and scuttling hermit shells, too cruelly cold
to swim, but how we stunned that azure sleep
of rage and icy water
to gasp and wallow on Atlantic stones
so cold and clean.

                  And how the green wood then
was wild with misdemeanors, every bush
screened some pursuit, and every forest pool
had country ritual, every crash in the trees
a panic of birds, or angels of the sense
embraced in air.

                How force went spendthrift then
and all our flowers were all for sale
for nothing all those days.

                    And now the year
as angry wood fights upward and explodes
from some old sense that festered in the ground.

*[103]*

## The Korean Mound at Peitaiho

On my North China Coast there grew a mound,
simply green ground
in a shape. When I was five years old
somebody told
me it held Korean ears. I forget all
the story, but some legendary Chinese general
so stored the trophies of his victory
deep in one bloody mound beside the sea;
and I could climb, sit, slide
all over this green disease
but knew what lay inside.
Now, buried under tons of years,
my eye of sense still sees
that mound coiled full of bright new shining ears.

[104]

## ODE FOR GERTRUDE ELY'S SPRING PARTY

Spring, never half so sweet as now nor ever half so sweet
again, now if never after, come spring come

with

tree trunks in pools of water, green rain and yellow willows,
daisy wheels and buttercups, meadowlarks and song-sparrows

with

milkmaids and shepherdesses, colin clouts and morris dances,
may rings and tennis balls, white shirts and boys running

with

broken hearts mended, wars hates and cares and fears forgotten,
green strength and careless love, lazy wits and shallow fancies,
spring, never half so sweet as now nor ever half so sweet
again, now if never after, come spring come.

*[105]*

# GOOD-BYE SUMMER GOOD-BYE GOOD-BYE

Like dolls on their little mile
of sand they walked, hand
closed on a finger of hand,
in a silent struggle of doubt
of the facts of love. And they did,
and they thought. And it all went out.
A tick of a watch, and it slid
and was gone for good and all,
though glance cut through glance and smile
and gray gaze to incise
love's effigy in the air
of the mind, fix there
forever the facts of eyes,
the skinfeel, the circumstance
of marriage, the stuff
of the act that slips away.
To remember will be enough
if they can remember today.

But it's gone, it won't stay.

The composition was hard:
the lighthouse, strict as a fact
on the dwindling spit, and the round
rock in the silver slip, and the packed
sand gritting the heel
of the hand, and the still pines
stuck in the rocks, and the sound
of the harbor buoy beating over
water, and gulls in the air
gray circles, and lover and lover
walking like dolls on their lines.

*[106]*

O pin, nail, fasten the pic-
ture hung in the gray of the mind,
if there's only a paper bag, a stick
of wood for tomorrow to find.

But it's all gone blind, gone blind.

No, out there, in a wheel
of gulls over the scum
on the gray water, it's real,
it's true, some-
thing tossing, a chip
in the tide, a splinter, a peel
of rind, or a sunk ship
floating a bone in the air.
It was real, it was true somehow,
it was there, it was there.
Gone in the gray now.

It's over, you can go now.

*[107]*

# APOLOGIES TO CRESTON

As I remember there were other travelers, too,
but no communication. At 2 p.m. and about 102°
there was a Burlington transcontinental in the station,

stainless steel, gleaming under noon gold. We, there alighting
from our tired Chevrolet, as at the wellside in the antique desert,
sought the oasis shade and the water; we, carrying

enough money to feed us and our car and get home
and no more; carrying the fragments of prairie travel, of last night
slept on the sidewalk in front of the church, next the weed patch,

somewhere nameless in Nebraska on US 6; now ventured
the little metropolis, and in the shining drugstore assimilated
glutinous malts and sundaes; and all about us the sweet-and-pretty

of a model town freshened, pressed starched and crisp, as for a wedding
or garden party; and we, shabby at the eyes from little sleep, not well
shaved, dry and hairy, foreign matter in their green lettuce.

How can we pick the towns and stops in the passage
of our life, stick each one like a bug on a pin, assemble
a string, and show them to our dinner guests? Yet of these stuffs are we made.

And even of ours, they; despite disapprovals; and if only
as something once under a fingernail, or combed out
of an eyebrow. No communication. But there we are.

Forward then toward evening, and the meal in the wayside weeds,
and the horse opera from the dashboard into late hours, which finally
tumbled us into the camp ground tented with boy scouts, somewhere near
        Keokuk,

and another day gone, and in the middle of it the unshared oasis.
Now on the map, unequivocally between Red Oak
and Chariton, find the name: Creston, Iowa: and hope we have not been
        rude.

[108]

# POUSSIN'S WORLD: TWO PICTURES

Here a young woman with no clothes on, mild,
marmoreal, hairless, handsome, dignified,
decants into an equally undressed child
(too young to walk, yet soon to be pie-eyed)
splashed wine. Elsewhere, one naked nymph, astride
a satyr piggy-back, points a stately hand
out of the picture toward some rout implied.
Design, not myth, made it. So the brain-land
Arcadia dreamed in paint. Neither the rose
smelled nor the sweat of actions in this June
of life's sweet counterfeit which art bestows.
Goats, gods, girls, and babies, blissfully immune
to dirt, fatigue, and morals, still compose
their own debauched, cherubic afternoon.

*[109]*

# ARMS AND THE MAN

Let us assemble the mediaeval man
at arms from the display in the show case;
here an armet, a sloped and snouted can
to help him keep his brains inside his face:
a lobster-plated gauntlet for the hand
which swung that ridged excruciating mace
cruelly couched on velvet. So, rise and stand,
bad baron in your steely carapace
invulnerable. But did no creepy grace
by breath of charm under green straw of hair
or white of the witch-eye leer upon your shield?
Could you stare down the gibber in a field
of germs, wash brains, or poison your own air?
*Povera bestia.* Just stand there and dangle your mace.

*[110]*

# THE ROMAN SOLDIER

Wearing some kind of iron hat, armed to the teeth with
whatever weapons are latest, he has stood in some square from
occupied Troy to now: seen from outside, monolithic;

dreaming inside of Vermont, or the Abruzzi, or Yorkshire,
or his father's boats tied at the jetty, or his girl in the grass,
or he's some slab without dreams, how do we know? Still less does he

know whether he's an angel with a sword or a fiend with a fork.
Somebody stuck him where he is, mostly among enthusiasts
who would hang him by the heels and spit on his head if they could.

If you upend the poor doll, its eyes will roll.
                                    Statuary
these figures are stationed across the colored countries and the years,
all much alike, but there has been no intercommunication.

[111]

# REMEMBER APHRODITE

Do you remember, Aphrodite, the sea
hours we had; sun gone green in water
lapping over knees; the stare of the offshore
boats at the beachward bodies bare
in the daystar beat and noon glare?
Do you remember arms hesitant, given,
squeezed in the sun; the long day divided between
us (o Aphrodite remember heaven);
hung between memory and fancy of future, in the still
air of our day owned in the sun and the sea?

Red froth, shameward parts of the body dismembered, blue
pain in the loins slapped out seaward, spittle
and waste in the slipwash grew
you at the fury of the heart enfoamed, chaste and bare,
o brittle divinity broken into beauty,
regathered there in the huge eyes, white stand,
dark-hair, rain-enwimpled grace
of girl imagined in brain eye and hand.

And oh, remember, Aphrodite, the shell
under your swimming feet, cool and all
alone on the long water. And lest our days
now in the gathering of gray, years drying on
us, gleam gone from the pools
and the light lost on the sea,
lest they inch us out and confuse, I hold the idol true
in the eye: so also you
deep in the hollow of your dream
Aphrodite remember me.

[112]

# NORTH CHINA AND THE CHILDREN

Pond country, and when willows in their pools
dream and loom back the trail and tress above
that weep, or as lily-pads where frogs squat plump
and dense, or where ducks cruise and color slats
of water, and all still ponds in all still forms
bring back the pavilion on the lotus-pool
and the painted bridge, the river and its drops
slid down and pearled from the bent oar that rowed
my father's boat, when I was five years old,
there where the bastion of the city wall
broke like some antediluvian stony ship
at Pao-ting-fu above the water-flowers.

Not one North China brat lives with his now
self as his own twin, nor as such whose first
home was not a rented temple, who does not know
that graves are pointed mounds of earth, that bricks
are baked in country kilns where you can find
dead babies if you dare look, who has not ridden
donkeys with bells on strings around their necks.
How can they live like us, if they came alive
by vitreous plumbing and grew strong among
sanitary odors? That man never smelled
who has not smelled North China in her pride.

This is no matriculation to the rear.
All we once children find the willowy pool,
splash down, pull the surface back in over us,
and douse in that green jelly where we were born.
The stone arch painted his own dream and form
as glaucous oval where the boat slid through
and the child's hand trailed in wonder and water-lily
stems. But this is the nursery, and the bed-time

milk, and the never-time of the fairy book
greenly enciphered in the stone-grown heart,
and not the year's content, only what squeezes out
in drops shining, but part of a piece of now.
I mean not China, only me and us.

We, once the dowered barbarian in the land,
the Goth on the capitol, dream now sadly back
as heirs to a kingdom gone. At Peitaiho
the mountains, the monastery cliff, and Buddha's
Tooth, and one inarticulate village lost
in a gulf of stone behind the Great Wall, portended
and met the sea, where Chinese fancy ended
in Lotus Hills and Tiger Rocks, against
the tea-and-cricket, the whiskey-soda names,
West End, East Cliff, Lighthouse Point, where the children
of missionaries and importers and the marines
dabbled their pale toes in the North China Sea.
How gone, how our feet stand now on no times.

Changelings with me remember what's no longer
ours, nor all enchantment. Once pneumonic plague
whitened the snowless freeze in the Gobi wind,
and dogs wrestled the top boards from their nails
on coffins for cold meat. The facts come home.
Not ours the beggar with no face, but think
how lady meant European, woman meant
Chinese, how we sat in rickshas and made
our runners race. They've pitched the Foreign Devils,
that's us, and fallen for new foreign devils,
worship the goblin Marx and the bannered face.
Little we deserved either, but let it be.
Some of them loved us when we were little, and we

loved them again, and the love that floats from a gone
amah-and-coolie world could still be love
that burns in blue above the festered corpse.

Children we shall not go back where they hauled
the nets in surf, seined flopping silvers, where thick
black boats were beached and roped to skinny anchors
that smelled of dead crabs under which the child
dried in his bliss, or where the diver slid
past the medusa steering her cold blobs
as azure emblems of a sea now lost.
And still the lighthouse gazes from the cliff
toward Chin-wan-tao, but we shall not come again
nor to the stone arch nor the lotus pond,
no more. But Chinese bells are in our heads.

Pond country is in my mind, and now at New Hope
the willows on the towpath, and all still
waters mean return, and five years old; they mean
green swimmings of the children, whose now here
floats on a scum of nowhere, but is theirs.

*[115]*

SPIDER

Bright captures, wing-shimmers, facts
of heart, sense, and fancy, as material
dreamed deep in my organs, anticipate
futures formed and radiant, when all
experience dissolves, desperate.

I eat my memories. Stomach stuff
of life is caught, shaped, and spread,
and what it was in the air,
gone from the flesh of thread
as form stays there.

Pearls and strings, rainwash, once
silent furies, now cling
quiet on heart-shapen leaves.
Spider does not sing,
only sits, sees, eats, and weaves.

*[116]*

# THE PROCESSION AND THE BOX: A TAPESTRY FOR VALENTINE

Now rides in the sweet silly season, and a progress
of armed shapes assembles on the frozen moor
out the window, and the year comes again, heartless
in steel plate. Open the box and shut the door.

What we have is here: our sometimes and our whens:
our nevers: hope caught in a jar: the girl on
the shell on the sea and the butterfly in the lens:
ropes in the arms: the face against the moon.

And outdoors, the riders pace at their season in bright rains
down stiff brown grass across a melting field.
Do we know them: strength, grace, hope: and what remains?
Oh, what red hearts we wear behind the iron shield.

*[117]*

# ANDRITSAINA REVISITED

The bus driver from Megalopolis had washed
his arms in wine, Karytaina castle dropped from sight behind
his elbow, and we saw Arcadia, eager to set up as new

the picture village of the mind from my forty-mile-a-day young-manhood,
a place of arbors and window boxes. But between times, andartes
and Nazis had played their games with it. There's something

in a bony hill town sucking on the blood of its past
that holds the inwards of you like a cold hand. We then,
lords of our little dollars, dried in the mouth over the goat-chops,

best these people could skin off the stones of their slopes;
and the pretty inn was gone somewhere unmentionable. At what was left,
we slept, and grumbled. Next day was given to Apollo's

house on the Bassai of the gray hillside, since not one
tourist ever went to Andritsaina for Andritsaina. It's the antiques.
And George, the drunken guide with the flower over his ear,

told us returning how, where we walked, resisters had stood the prodotes
in a line and gunned them into open graves, with Christos Christopoulos
the lordly and gentle innkeeper of the days of my youth.

Nazis were bad: who else good, who bad, my God, who knows now?
There had been women singing once as with hammers they broke
stones, long ago, to make the new road. It is not yet finished.

And still the grace is there in street faces and the bones of the people.
Andritsaina offered a scrubby flower plucked from the hillsides
of the days of all our freshness before the world was made so evil.

*[118]*

# THE CRABS

There was a bucket full of them. They spilled,
crawled, climbed, clawed: slowly tossed
and fell: precision made: cold iodine color of their own
world of sand and occasional brown weed, round stone
chilled clean in the chopping waters of their coast.
One fell out. The marine thing on the grass
tried to trundle off, barbarian and immaculate and to be killed
with his kin. We lit water: dumped the living mass
in: contemplated tomatoes and corn: and with the good cheer of civilized
     man,
cigarettes, that is, and cold beer, and chatter,
waited out and lived down the ten-foot-away clatter
of crabs as they died for us inside their boiling can.

*[119]*

# DETAILS FROM THE NATIVITY SCENE

Crèche star and lit tree,
bells in the snow
every year
model the nativity
and show the holy family
and all its angels near
before they go.

Begin with arrangement. Protagonists
who are, but did not act, serene in the center
stage, and either side half-choruses. To the left
the shepherd thralls, a congregation of gray lumps,
embarrassed in nailed boots and coarse hoods, shuffle
their feet, and worship dumbly. On the right, lordly
philosophers dedicate with grace their whatevers
of perfumery and jewels. The middle triad is man
mother baby: representing the virtues, as honesty
devotion, and yet again some humanity still not fixed
in the stream of perception: a future; an icy bud
sealing beyond the world's imagination the tangible
dream to come. Behind, hardly seen, tame animals
breathe and gaze.

     Outside in the street, snow falling.
A few loungers. Also, significant of the world of power:
which holds, but is excluded from a history
it knows is happening: the mercenaries loiter
on their spears: hostile.

Why was it first shepherds? They, on the stony
slope at night: lonely but grouped: not owning
in full the animals they watched: not cunning
beyond the strategy of the wolf and the sheepstealer:

bored and tired: who possessed never any youth
you could call youth. See, this is what the choruses of satyrs
attendant on the year-spirit's birth are become
in our time. With imagination but without words,
how could they see deliverance from the wind
and the watching, the ephemeral coziness
of the leather bottle, except as they did see it?
Fireworks, that is, and gaudy gentlemen
in wings and wheels of light and glares of clothing
who blew trumpets at them, and spoke, loud but kind,
and invited them in to the circle of the privileged.

And on the day when these shall slip their essence
of sturdy gray for sheer weft and fluid
shall it be into what they imagined as lords of the world?
To this there is not yet any answer we know.
Only, that there was never again so bleak
an air on the stony slope, after such apparitions.

Next had come the wise Kings: young men, strong
and thoughtful: possessors already: and the imagination
of their dreams were simple figures of holding. Therefore
they gave, so that the gleam in the gift might be given
them to keep: in giving, asking then. One said:
I know that every sack has a small hole.
Where I climb no goat can go, where I swim no fish
follow; what squeezes on the heel of the hand
is sweet for resistance to the shoulder behind,
and the force blown headlong into exhaustion is a glory.
I am so strong and wonderful, but I can count,
and when I have to begin to be careful, what shall I do
then?
    The next said: The world is a magnificence in my eye.
But what shall I do, Lord, to store my possessions?

[121]

How can I keep the fern under the pine, and the gulls'
wings silvering flight on blue water, how seize
and hold the long green hills? My eye would devour them
and grasping, worship, for what is religion, but every
man trying to fasten the fluid of his lovely youth that escapes
and paint his glory forever on one sweet day?
Death I hate, not so much bones in coffin as when
the wave shall break or the leaf spin down
red, and I am there, and do not notice.
Captures escaping wash always the young sense fresher
but when the dear wish to capture is gone, then
Lord, what shall I do?
                              The third said: He has become
I, for in the spoiling of muscle and sense-shock
the mind is left, and plump or husked, here the abstract
tissue of inward is more beautiful than body
or bone even: the structure of God in the proposition.
Materials are necessary, organs and coil of bowels,
soapy brain or blood's broth. Some odd slimes
make these flowers of thought. If they dry,
petals crumble. Yet, death I fear not. It can be reasoned.
What do I need with teeth, hands, or parts, or courage?
But, Lord, when the visible cord of connection
slips in the vise, will not hold, I tell you, when I
can no longer follow proof to proof,
then, Lord, oh Lord, what shall become of me?


I do not think any answer was given at the time.
It was more likely in some off hour of the next
night: jogging the way home:
tired, in ordinary weather, a dry star or two
up there, but no more rockets or glory: camels
grunting and clanking: conversation at a fag end,

and gone, each man alone. One saw
the sinew on the rack, the wonderful force,
dying on the tree speared helpless petering out
in the icon of the imagination behind his eye.
He remembered how certain barbarous people would not
let a pubic boy be one of the men until
he had killed a bear. The village caught a cub and fed it
huge: chained him: the growing boys one after one
blooded their spears: they cut off his head and nailed it
over the village hall and prayed to it: Great bear
give us your hairy strength, o bear, let us be warriors.
But what if the bear's head answered: You have used me.
Your innocence is gone, you have not cared
for what it is to be a bear. What is strength?
I am a dry head, you are sick.
                    One saw
a man holding an open sack and the dollars dropped in
and jangled: the blessing and the beauty
of the company of love sold and paid for.
He dreamed of signing a check for the winsome
collocation of properties of the world
he had made his in a garden for his own bride.
He saw caterpillars eating leaves of his tree,
flies dying on his pond, and clotted the shining, and the girl
mumbled between decayed teeth stories of outright
possession and whoredom, and he stood in the shoddy ferns
holding his money.
                    One heard, in another garden,
the cry of the mind's pain, doubt of faith, crippled
understanding, the awful why? And he saw a blackboard written over
with judgments, and the only one that made any sense
said a = a.

*[123]*

After such dreaming they spoke
together, saying: Surely, we are nowhere near our answers
but it is plain we shall not reach them single
nor by the three of us only. Saying also:
What stuffs we gave were too much less than our askings,
and: Our strong acts fail until we forget the actor.
We are broken coins of each other, whose ragged edges
without our match simply eat air. Do you
remember, the other side of those three, some stuffing
of lumpish shapes? Is there some glimpse there
of God we have not seen? But what were those three
we were called, star-steered, magnetized
to their worship? Was it a real baby? We
have been told of the year-spirit, the child
of the breath of thunder in the body of the girl
who is a blossom split from the dreaming clod.
Yet we hope these are not gods. Of gods, we have heard:
wise and strong, but being perfect they must overpower
us, or we defy them. Surely it begins
not with God, that is too far beyond us,
but in our fathers or our children, in our people
to whom we belong and of whom we are a part
as they of us and belong. There it may come.
So, riding in the ruins of their pride,
puzzled and hope-starred still the shining kings
have left the stage.

        Both choruses have gone.
Now the protagonists rose and left their places
in flight before the final element
of this morality: the titans or the satyrs,
the supernumeraries of the world of power
facing loss. They came in pikes and jacks.

[124]

They had the village hooped. Streets crossed and fouled
on armors and despair, and swords were out
and poking. There were screams. Aloof, secure
the woman in her blue hood rode her beast
and held the sleeping baby whose calm weight
dreamed on the saddle as the bearded man
plodded beside. Back in the snow, steel reeked.
The foundering henchmen gibbered on their loss.
Where is the king? Where is the tyrant child?
Where is the bud from thunder and the nymph
born with his crown askew in the green vines?
Oh, where are our lost afternoons displayed
in careless love, our elderly pursuits
in the hot grass? Where is the infant king?
Their fury strangled in the bloody dark.
The sound died, and the echoes were lost in the snow.

So all are gone. But every year
the child comes. The simple see
the lit tree
the angels and the gifts and glory.
Every year
the winter story
plays. The spirit hovers near
in wise brains that know
their own unwisdom, how gifts change and go.
But every year
the child is here
in the ceremonial tree
bells in the snow
until the day even we
in the night shall know
and see
who we are and where we go.

## GHOST OF NO FLESH REMEMBERED

Sweet fiction, flown now as material
in motion, now a shape made out of airs
and graces, you are heard along the hall
in songs, as footsteps up and down the stairs,
or, child, you are composed where arm and hand
lie in the vine's spilled shade along the floor,
or form from gloom of window panes to stand
and question shadows in the corridor.
Fragrance where flowers were none, echoes from where
no music made, o child, you lived from sight
as one small grace imagined on the air
who shrank to hide from the invading light,
but when the switch is turned you still are there
sucking your finger at my door all night.

[126]

# THE WATCHES

Bed time as rain time drenched the homeward cars
who wiped and shifted at the corners, black
swam gold by haloed trees, wet lamps, flooded
shutters in glories, till they ebbed and drained
in rained-out hush, and the flat face of the land
turned toward an air now drying, in whose hole
of sucked-in silence at the mile-off yards
came locomotive time, and monsters barreled
in black walked out their furies, threw fits
of noise in pistons and reversed and stamped
their herds to silence; hooting, one long freight
puffed out into the prairie; on the void
came time of tick and tock and the loud clock
spoke through it and told how the unslept eyes
are cubicles for shabby transients, how
the brain ticks out nocturnal silence; now
gray seas softly stormed window panes, and there,
streets off, the milk-horse clopped his chips of noise
where hopped the morning rabbit on that grass
which makes the dewy time of oystershell
and hush filled with the rabbit and the horse
before tired sheets were thrown, and the night blind
came up to show, by grass and picket fence,
the world of the green walls, the backyard leaves
rainstrung and sweet from night and sung with birds
and dried in gold as the hot day came in.

*[127]*

## DAISY NONSENSE

She loves me she loves me
not in the white wheel and
fall, in the picked held and the
dropped petals; in watery
wind and blown weather she
loves me, and dry seasons
dry and she loves me
not in the stiffening
stalk time; on brown after-
noons, think of long green
hours, through the cream-
y stripping of daisies she
loves me she loves me
not in the think times of
time, but in day time.

*[128]*

# COLLAGES AND COMPOSITIONS

Use force and chisel, be lapidary, not
any cut-

stone-arranger. Fear finished counters. Take
splinters, make

grammar out of nails, paper, rubber bands
placed by hands

bemused, rags, pins, a piece of string,
anything

but ready-made lovely matters: Flowers,
whose rapt hours'

arranging builds on material
glory al-

ready shaped and sweet: pebbles: snow-
flakes are no

stuff. Not perfections. Only broken stones,
potsherds, bones,

scraps of felt pinched in a wire vise
can surprise;

or willful sense flash taken wrong:
half bird song

misremembered, shining phrase reworded
not recorded,

used, abused, retaken from the cannibal heart:
this is art.

[129]

# THE PILLOW AND THE BOOK

About a thousand years ago,
sick for lost love, sleepless alone I lay
from red dayfall through black to morning gray
trying to read *Ulysses* in a borrowed room
while yesterday's rejections played their act below
the ecstasies of Molly Bloom,

and the intolerable gray page
of print, in timeless nonsense, beat my eyes to mock
a lonely universe of sheets and clock
where I, king in an empty house and a night
cohabited by solitude and rage,
killed time into daylight,

and then got up, and left the place,
and never set eyes upon that furniture
again of white-night torment. O all poor
adolescents, what unsleeps you must endure, to span
with literature and life that deadly space
between the boy and man.

*[130]*

# A SIDING NEAR CHILLICOTHE

From the high deck of Santa Fe's El Capitan
cabs, sand-domes, stacks were seen above the box-car line:
old locomotives parked, antediluvian

in cruel progress, gone before us to that night
toward which we, sacks of memories, slide in blander airs,
and streamline our old eyes and thoughts from glass and flight.

Our ears, boys' ears, and eyes and hearts were haunted by
huge hoots of laughter down the dark: the glow: the steam
bulging in black and red up the spark-shot sky.

Now wheels, rails rust together, dews and sunshine eat
the iron grace: through silence their corrosion ticks
and drops in red dust, junk of grandeurs obsolete.

So, like old elephants who stumbled off to die
in their known place and rot their bulks from ivory bones,
the locomotives stood against the prairie sky.

[131]

# GREEN AND WHITE

*From and to Horace*

Who sipped your drinks and saw Soracte bald with snow,
knew love sweet still, but knew too well how love's delight
goes where good Valentino and sweet Marilyn go
out at the cluttered dusty other end of night . . .

In which same night, this side, Horatius, I can see
the moths of hands and face make moments in the dark;
have my sweets still, but head gains over heart in me:
an elder wed to his Susanna, senior clerk

on legs as green as heron's, but the molting owl
glares from under my hat. Cut me and I'll still bleed.
But that thick pulse is watering into wit and soul
and reminiscence. Mine own vapors. Take no heed,

you by the hedge, and you who softly stroll and sit
and giggle in the half dark. Seize perfections, know
how the green time is still your own. Make use of it.
We did. I never thought how you could move me so.

*[132]*

# KING FOR A DAY

No seed grew in the ground that year.
　　That year no blade was seen.
The water sank in the dusty ground
　　and no green tree was green.

And with dry hearts and brains of salt
　　we hated the world we saw,
and neighbor stole from his neighbor's hoard,
　　and no man knew the law.

The stone was dry in the spirit grove.
　　The high gods heard no prayer.
The doubtful sphinx coiled in our hills
　　and sickened all our air.

Then the Old Man came from the mountain side,
　　down from the fields of snow,
with his stick and his beard and his dirty coat
　　and the wisdom of long ago.

He told what songs to sing at the ground,
　　what ribbons to hang on the tree,
and the wines to make and the kegs to break,
　　and the rituals to let be,

and how to break the doom of the world
　　and crack the fate in the glass
by setting back wisdom a hundred years
　　and nature to where it was.

He made us dream on the youth we lost
　　and the young dreams lost before,
when the memory-tree is green in the mind
　　with leaves that it never wore.

[133]

He bounced the dance on the country green,
  and aped the teacher and priest,
and kicked the sergeant, and mocked the mayor,
  and drove the cook from the feast
and the young grew wise and the old grew young
  and the great was less than the least;

and the high gods reeled on their thrones of ice
  as the red wine ran like rain,
and the rags dropped free of the Old Man's skin
  and his sinews were young again,

and the blood pumped in the dry of the veins
  and arm and fist swelled strong
and bright for never and white for now
  and beautiful for not-long.

For the man or maid who goes to the stone
  goes garlanded and gay
like groom or bride in pomp and pride
  with flowers along the way,
and the white bull dies with gilded horns
  upon his wedding day.

He ogled the girls, and chose his bride,
  and kissed her there in the light,
and hooked her waist in his giant arm
  and swept her into the night.

Nobody knows what went on in the hay
  and what went on in the clover,
but we found him asleep at the break of day,
  and the day-king's day was over.

[134]

We took him away to the private glade
    and the spiritual stone,
and stood him up, and broke in his head,
    and lopped him bone from bone,

and carefully sowed the reeking bits
    in the fields for miles around,
and the spirit worked in the rotting blood,
    and the seed grew in the ground;

and the fields turned sweet with glory of grain,
    and the young folk walked between
singing softly in the new rain,
    and all the new year was green.

*[135]*

# WELLHEAD

Alone with verse I made once, I, father and blood spring suffer
haunt-wings and tease and flitter of spirits. These I have made, these
dream in paper, they are: what fingers and bone, what brain, what fat
of the loin, what lust of the eye made, these make now (undersleep
moves still memory of unseen): bug-wings glimmer and flitter
as rhyme and word-host calling me father. Alone with what I
made and an making I, the red pump, pump, and as gnats' thin wings
whine, and hovercloud haunts me, the paper indestructible
universe, that is I and my poems, mimes out the no-world.
Over the wellhead wings whir and glimmer.

*[136]*

## PROBLEMS OF DISPOSAL

Again and again up there the apothecaries combining
ingredients repeat their reciprocal series
of experiments: shaking loose on the dance floor, at the community

pool the combinations of futures: soft looks, the connubial
expression in the eyes: it means squeeze, germination, cramming
the lovely confusion till there's no room, no room. Presently

room's made in a hotter kind of chemistry: holocausts
happen in hate: messes occur: red collisions, whenas
it becomes compulsive to sponge and wipe up certain congestions

on the bleeding globe. So 1914 1939 19 when?
Captivate and create, undo, clean up, and begin it
again. But if upstairs the apothecaries, bugging

their abominable eyes over the crucible, become
aware that material has eaten its own tissue, no more
combinations will ensue? One only surmises that, learning

nothing, they will pick up the apparatus and try it all again,
    elsewhere.

*[137]*

## EARLY APPLES

All week they had fallen, while on stones and grassed
ground we knelt to the circle of the tree
to gather hard bright balls, and at the last
it was down to weak blobs, leaking filthily

colored juice like chewed tobacco. So I stand
under the tree and rage at time and God
palming the wet brown smell in my clean hand.
O future, future. High above, the proud

shape towers to green still sowr with rounded gold,
like some lost sight of the Hesperides'
domain. The world was apple. Pale and cold
our ciders juiced in such tight balls as these

before their rot, and shapes of innocence
and fresh delight were apples that grew young.
Globes were the skins of all experience
firming the damp pith, yellow sap, and strong

brown-buttoned stem and core, to show and be
the story of love undone, foul death foreplanned
where Eve stood in her hair beneath the tree
and held the bitten apple in her hand.

*[138]*

# THE BIRDS ACROSS THE SEA

The names of birds are near
heart's heritage in our lines of song and story.
They will not leave our minds. These names are here,
and on these pages painted in their glory
the book-writ birds appear.

*Wryneck,* by foredone
or lovesick maidens fastened on a wheel
and turned by night and hidden from the sun
by day, and sung by moonlight, thus to steal
back the beloved one:

jynx torquilla, brown, barred,
and with the woodpecker's long toes to use
for climbing. He's Ixion the ill-starred
who rides his jinx-wheel, by the hand of Zeus
for love flung far and hard.

*Bustard,* once annoyed
by Xenophon's men on the Euphrates plain,
who ran wtith feet uplifted and employed
his wings like sails, and was not seen again.
Alone upon the void

the black *Imperial*
*Eagle* uses one head, yet once he knew
prerogatives of the armorial,
and on a Habsburg blazon he wore two.
Grandeur for him was all.

*[139]*

*Lapwing*, that Benedick's
Beatrice ran like. *White Stork*, long of life
and leg, who nests among the chimney sticks
and stones, and flies the baby to the wife
in spite of all our tricks.

*Skylark*, whose simple song
stirred Shelley into several thousand words,
though Huxley's D.H. Lawrence thought it wrong
to switch him from the company of real birds
into the angelic throng

that poet was so prone
to find himself projected in. There are
a few who see in birds the overtone
of Unseen Presences moving from afar,
not just the bird alone;

for instance, Wordsworth, who
from birds in general saw intimations
of immortality for himself, and knew
only some transcendental implications
within the name *Cuckoo*.

*Fieldfare*, once greedily
dined on by Cleopatra (that's from Shaw).
*Nightjar*, beloved of John Galsworthy,
looking most like a drowsy pile of straw
or whippoorwill to me.

*[140]*

From Thracian fairy tale
King *Hoopoe*, helmet crested, striped of wing;
*Swallow*, not here of barns; with her, a pale
brown sister bird condemned to grieve and sing,
the fabulous *Nightingale*

from prehistoric haze
of myth who bubbles still her tale of wrong,
the bright and bloody thread caught in a maze
of moonlight woods and legendary song
to haunt us all our days.

*Kingfisher*, not as here
shock-headed, but streamlined from beak to wings
to bolt his blue dive down the atmosphere,
whose nesting stills the winter sea and brings
the halcyon time of year.

Names, names of birds. Always where
books will be read and stories still will be
remembered, in a not too festered air,
bright and so literate for all to see,
the birds will still be there.

*[141]*

*A Field Guide to the Birds of Britain and Europe,* by Roger Tory Peterson, Guy Mountfort, and
P.A.D. Hollom (Houghton Mifflin). With gratitude.

## AMERICAN NIGHTS

### 1

This is a world of picket fences, knowing
the girls pass arm in arm from up the courthouse square
down to the soda parlor, hears them throwing
the fragments of their laughter down the dark
and summer-close and elm-grown small town air.
The bandstand in the middle of the park
watches lank adolescents swing their cars
with languid fingers into cruel curves,
reverse and start and wipe the night with stars,
and take the road, this ribbon world of nerves
driving forever driving in a dream
of black escape from automobile eyes.
On either hand the backward landscapes stream
as flight in fluid haste, and memory-wise.

### 2

A fallen column overgrown with grass:
a U-shaped lyre bestrides it, and the bust
of a baroque musician in a wig
observes your steps upon this antique dust.
A broken angel with a dizzy smile
invites you in; and did you know how big
flowers in our heart the classic world, the style
of swans in lakes, tutu and entrechat
and figure manual by Petitpas?
The lonely cemetery of the heart
grows on its graves and in its cracks of stones
such blooms as break the granite shells apart
where reminiscent ballerinas start
out of the sweet arrangements of our bones.

### 3

Knee deep in froth of daisies and the night,
you found the house, haunted the window light

thinned by drawn shade, and wetly stood and spoke:
"Let me back in, since I lived here before."
Your black key sickened in the lock and broke.
You could not force the door.
Steps sounded in the house and went away.
The moon came out and bleached a broken gate
where too much grass had grown. All you could do
was wait, count your lost pulse, watch the moon climb,
and try the hopeless door again, and wait,
while this night scene of all you could not do
enciphers you into the rest of time.
The story is not finished. This is you.

### 4

Noon sharpened every outline that you saw,
the braided sinews on the drawbridge gates,
the prison guard, rapt in his tower of glass,
the tarns of ice engraved with sticks and skates,
crows in the frozen cocks of harvest straw,
the tanks of heaters, stacked and stripped of gas,
white smoke, stopped on the blue, as frozen fleece.
Riding the slipstream to the edge of sight
it does not flow but slides in all one piece
back from the tunnel where you clipped the light
in snapping shears of stone and lost your day.
But lost is won nor gone is gone away.
All arching splinters of this day remain
and reassemble in the pondering brain.

### 5

Now day's bright angers glitter in the skull.
The lightless outer air is squeezed away
and makes a coffin of our wheeling hull
for these two hours as, lit within, and thrown
in the wrong way

and inside out from headlong panes, the play
of shadows gives ourselves to us, and mocks
our ghosts in glass, the slogans in a line
of platitudes below the roof, and rocks
the idiotic sisters on their sign.
Here in our small sealed universe we breathe each other's air,
companionless companions of the train.
We are the uncommunicated thoughts who stare
and jostle, cooped inside one iron brain.

#### 6

Cased in such brains, the swarming parts of me
turned and grew inward, monads of the mind,
and as they died, each in his private, blind,
unwindowed consciousness, mold and leaf rot
worked in the reminiscence of the sense
and germinated in the iron pot.
I grow in my own landscape like a tree.
The glory shapes inside the grass-grown fence.
I wear this rainbow wash of dreams that make
a false imperium of pride, rehearse
my splendors in a cruel travesty, and shake
the helpless sovereign in his universe.
That thing is I. But what I try to be
I am not. What I am, I can not see.

#### 7

Here stands the town, our castles in its trees
by whose dark involutions lie embraced
our rights and tithes, our franks and baronies.
Its theme, our lives, escaped in wheels and haste:
its streets, our parish where dreams feed like sheep:
the 1860 general in the square:
the flat boat on the river mud asleep:
the depot stranded in its ties and steel:
the stations of our time in everywhere.

The midnight park where sweethearts clasp and kiss
in leafy corners makes the witness moon
accomplice to our metamorphosis.
Our own eyes light behind the window frames
as bulbs and shades, and shine as private flames.

8

A pole of spine, a hatch of sticks and strings,
a cage of nerves hook up, suspend, and shore
my treasury of vapors, winds, and heat.
Somewhere in this neat wilderness there sings
the miniature of an angelic mind.
Inside the wall a whole wonderful wide
creation in full sovereignty maintains
the soft interior of pulps and veins.
Illuminated memory inside
this rhetoric of flesh, this more than meat
of physiology, grows inward wings.
In me and nowhere else the world is grown.
By which dear mess of waters, salts, and fats
my germ walks singing through its frame of slats.

9

The gift of giving countermands the loss.
Me: you: the boundaries blend, our private nights
with all their starry populations cross.
I give you mine with all its rents and rights.
If on the backs of graves we kissed and held,
the flimsy specters dallied in their sheets.
The driven progress of our flight compelled
fond fresh conjunctions in our midnight streets.
Sometimes such lonely spheres, adrift and blind,
wearing their glories in a sconce of bone,
trespass on miracles and wake to find
through soft collisions that they are not alone.
Dear love, take in my vase of star-grown flowers.
The door is open and the house is ours.

## SHRIKE

As executioner, he wears
a mask across his eyes, and tears
his prey with hooky beak, and cares

nothing for victims' pains or cries;
impales his meat before it dies
on barbs and thorns against the skies.

He stocks his larder thriftily,
carnivorous almost as we,
a careful baron in his tree,

the terror of each smaller thing
that flies and nests. And in the spring
he falls in love and tries to sing.

*[146]*

# UNWELCOME THRIFT ON JUDGMENT DAY

How, when all we who breathe are stopped and sown,
compost to feed the nerves of grass and grain,
shall all the thoughts that bulge against the bone,
the wishes from the cocoon of the brain
half-winged for bright escape, be gathered back
while angry angels bugle home the yield
of all the world's best time, and stoop to hack
our reputations from their reeking field?
Domed of our joints and blood, our books and lines
of grace in shapen stone, our works of art
and civic strength, the city of heaven shines:
manifest future. And this heretic heart
resents his imperfections all denied.
Green grew the buds damned when the old tree died.

*[147]*

## FLOWERS AND THORNS IN THEIR TIME

Roses cloud my arms in green, stick
and hurt; red climbs from stalk and water, flying
suckers arch; shears lop vain heads, my hands
bag and stack the lost splendors. Roses
hurt, delight, make me think of dying.

Roses, too sudden, dramatize
my birth and bud, scarlet and astonishment, in steep array
among the greens, rains, thorns, my
pride, spiky postures of defense, farewell
favors, fading glory, sweet decay.

Where where in rose time find some way
to keep and fasten, hold forever in the hurt
heart this June pain and passion? See
from dead-colored wood green wood swells: for other Junes of roses
spermy future updriven from the deep dirt.

*[148]*

# MOURNING DOVES

Soft and startled out of wind carven slopes, the prairie lights
run them up and out in wind and sun, paired flights
of doves, fluid on the dry, as flying tails, browns and whites,

Utah to Connecticut two by two identical,
paired in flight, or modelling high breasted sweet symmetrical
sentimental shapes along the wires of country fence rail.

Wild mourning doves are all alike. Urban rock pigeons breed
hybrid multicolored gang-grouped citizens, they wheel and feed
in squares and parks, man-wise, dainty, vain, full of greed,

and no two alike. Messy marriers. City pigeons coo
but garble calls with mongrel-sorted colors.
                                        Two by two
identical to shape and in their little whoop and hoo hoo hoo

wild morning doves are constant lovers ever to themselves and to their nature
    true.

*[149]*

## THE PAINTER'S EYE

Flags hang on the wall
limp as winds fall.
Barons stand blank and tall.

Dragons sleep in a school
of coiled wings, and cool
their mail in the garden pool.

Sweethearts fly in the air.
Angels sit on the stair
and comb their bright hair.

Unicorns in full view
graze groves and fields through.
The trees are blue.

Hand heavy, eyes of lead,
the king sleeps on his bed.
Dreams fill the white head.

*[150]*

# REMORSE

The snake tooth pinches his own mail:
the rabid dog fox bites his foot:
cancerous claw and scorpion tail
turn inward and self-rend. Brute

crab in the box eats the lung.
He tears the fact, unmakes the made.
The pelican, who feeds his young
on his own flesh by flesh betrayed,

reverses beak to split the wound,
bites on the sack and pulls it through,
throws heart and vitals on the ground
to prove that heart, at least, was true.

*[151]*

# EASTER

Our April is the lamb who died
to paint the year in tones of pride
blown where the lamb was crucified.

The lamb was slaughtered where he stood.
They nailed the lamb across the wood.
They carved the lamb and boiled his blood.

How shall we pack our sins of pride?
The ruffling soldiers lounged and eyed
the carcass of the lamb who died
and speared the water from his side.

The glory of the year has grown
from where they buried the unknown
lamb in a hole beneath the stone.

Lilies blown in soft airs repeat
the victim killed, the lamb to eat,
the heart and entrails dressed as meat.

How could the time transform him so?
How did the lamb make April grow?
The lily and the blood root know.
They drank his blood beneath the snow.

*[152]*

# FAILURE

How did it come ungathered, all the sheaved throng
of graces and good-byes? Dandelion-blown in the strong
wind, time's spindrift-whirling pressures, our young

moment of together and yesterday flies
the storm. The date enacts and dies.
How can I hold the look in your eyes?

How pull and store thistledown out of the blast?
It slipped, air-caught, at the last.
Sweet wind, sweet wind, where have you blown our past?

[153]

## THE FIRST SEVEN YEARS

That was a time of furniture and family
and books and gramophones and happiness
and afternoon and servants and late tea
and lamps, my mother in a trailing dress,
the vases on the mantel white and blue,
the cat asleep along the window sill.
Our Victor with the morning-glory horn
held Farrar and Caruso in its walnut case
and bugled Marguerites and Butterflies.
The rainbow fairy books by Andrew Lang
with Eisenkopf and princesses forlorn
displayed their simple magics to my face.
The antiques of the heart can spell me still.
That wood was haunted and the bluebird sang.

*[154]*

# DECEMBER FRAGMENTS

I thought of cards along the mantelpiece,
the fire of logs, the stockings on the wall,
the team of deer, the cotton beard, the sleigh,
the ox and donkey munching winter hay,
the sleeping doll beside the floodlit stall,
shepherds and lambs in imitation fleece,
the sentimental chimney and the chair,
tin horns on earth and fireworks in the air,
peace and good will. Dear trash, I loved you so.
I thought of stars and bulbs and tinsel strings,
angels in curling pins, with paper wings,
bells of spun glass, and drifts of mineral snow.

[155]

# SAINT DEMETRIUS AND SAINT GEORGE

Twin iconographies. The two young horsemen rear
their mounts above two fallen dark antagonists.
Each has his victim stuck on a down-driven spear.
St. George has pinned a dragon form who flails and twists
in snakish sprawl. Demetrius in the other frame
kills an unhappy looking bearded warrior.
Rider spear prey: the composition is the same.
Our fiends their fallen, and our saintly calendar
their acts, their history our hope, and still they ride
against the reptile rancor and the armored force
of fury, martyr and knight-errant side by side.
Each spears his destined terror from a heaving horse.
Dimitri I. The outer Frank or Turk lies still.
The poisonous snake's inside, too hard for me to kill.

*[156]*

# THE KRANKENHAUS OF LEUTKIRCH

The forest nuns, who sheltered us and healed
with charms and science our unfinished frames,
spelled us with some effluvium of the sense
from their own childhoods' wonderment concealed
behind the robe, the veil, the snowy shield.
We knew no tongues; we only knew their names,
identities, and smiles, could not communicate.
Yet all is of a piece; some essence still comes through
from the house, the sisters, and, outside the gate,
the gloom, the wizard world of pines, the great,
the haunted and inhabited and enthralled
interminable Württembergerwald,
and I remember what I never rightly knew,
as in a harbored memory, not quite mine,
that German mind whose gothic dreams divine
the Kobold of the stream, the burnished ritterling,
the sylvan witch who sings behind her door,
the chilly jungfrau of the sevenfold spring,
and psychic manikins who with folded wing
sit on the mushroom circles of the forest floor.

[157]

## ANASTYLOSIS

They waken the weed-grown drums from their sprawl of death, pile up
columns, rebuild the anatomy of parthenons, with white plaster
caulk the cracks, new marbles are boned into the holes in the temples.

Persephone, Koré, doll of death in the iris, pupilla
butterfly-winged as psyche floating in the dust of the subter-
ranean hive above the squirming ribbon of snake; arid

is your transit: peaches wrinkle, apples blear in the salt wind,
oases shrink upon their cities and springs run sand.
Arrogant your return from the putrid sleep in the boneyard.

And houses die before the bulldozer, crumbled and carted
off, men work in the slats of doors to nowhere, naked
pipes are nucleus to the new nightmare of concrete uprising.

Some poison pains the physics of the dust to reassemble
and lust to sprout and writhe, and the potash cities rankle
as weeds in the living desert. Your April, Persephone,

resurrects in your walking. In hair spun and piled like butter,
mouth pouting, eyes like eggs, juice in all the tubes and the bulges
tight, the proud doll trips on four-inch heels down the marble sidewalk.

*[158]*

# THE MACEDONIAN CHAMBER TOMB

My idiot's glory. Privacy conceals
the solitude of his confines who feels
only his roof eggshelled above and cracked
for life to fester in, the germ of addled fact.
Build me a dome
and break it. Such is my eternal home.
And in this buried belfry who but the bat,
that filthy mouse with wings who acts the soul,
sleeps off his fidgets hanging by his heels?
It only needs a hole
in the head for life to mold and rot the brain.
Sun breaks now in the roof-hole. None so brave
as this imbrained stone-hatted world of mine
where the chambered girl dreams through her golden rain,
and Plato's solipsists all in a line
chained to their endless television pine
for sky, and pull the world inside their cave.

[159]

# THE INTERVAL

The roon half lived in, the two beds, and one
is empty, and our clock guarding the shelf
wakes only me. I hold this shell of time,
this bubble of being, and am half myself,
and feed on fragments, charm the hours with rhyme.
Room, my arterial castle, how undone
you are through loss in being only mine.
Memory sleeps in my arms and I wake up
to the white imagination in the sheets
and cold promise of past. The filtered blinds
of dawn, the roosters heard far off, the streets
breathing sweet recent rain bring back the cries
that woke our sleeps together, when the world
was in one piece, and I could see your eyes.

*[160]*

# A LODGING FOR THE NIGHT

Verona was always arduous. The station is colossal
and next to nowhere. No room in any hotel, they told us.
We stood stupidly in the vast halls, and the train was gone

into midnight. A fat dubious man and a sober thin one
murmured, it's the opera season, but spoke of a lodging,
bellissima, altogether respectable. They teetered the suitcases

on the handlebars of a bicycle. Walking half in our sleep
we trailed them past silent crowds of men sitting asleep on
baggage, or brushing their teeth into the empty cabstand.

We dreamed along dead beat down the bright enormous
desolate street. From a café a woman in a Garbo raincoat
got up and followed us a few steps shaking her head. It all came

out of some modern Italian movie. We shambled under
a gate, across a court. There was a clean shabby hallway,
an old woman and a little girl. I have no idea where they

slept. Our chamber was huge, the bed eight feet
wide, and hard as we lay and watched where on the dresser
across the room, a doll, large as a child, staring with solemn

eyes, waved forever still in the air her waxen expensive fingers.

*[161]*

# MEMORY OF A SCHOLAR
## (W.A.O. 1880–1945)

I set this down. Magister, can it be?
How shall I shape the wind that once was you?
Fancies seduce the memories in me.
This must be true, though nothing else were true.
I dared not praise you when you were alive.
Not I. You would have blown me off my feet
with stormy courtesy, the roar of wit
hiding the old Greek dread of godlike praise
for living men. But how shall verse contrive
your presence? Wave, my wand. So I recall
a Wilamowitz seen as Buffalo Bill,
Boeckh on a bicycle, and with it all
a better bibliographer by far
than any of your German idols. Now I see
the calligraphic hand, the blacksmith's bust,
the Civil War commander's brusque imperial,
the calvary moustache, the chin upthrust,
the big bold pipe, the bolder black cigar,
the paleographer's fastidious eye.
You, my professor, you before my face
unrolled the script of scholars, put in place
Traube and Vahlen, Leo, Reitzenstein,
and set the stars for all our lives to steer them by.
Your force was schooled to skills, the leonine
turned lapidary; syntax and the line
at fault and needing surgery brought to bear
the steely grammar shaped in pain and care.
You mounted on minutiae to aspire
with Plato up the staircase of ideas
and ranged, a ruler, all his cloudy sky,
and came back down to his deep cave with light and heat
in worlds where men see dust and you saw fire,
to blow your edicts from your chair at ease,

Jupiter of the seminar benign
with poets nuns and Baptists sitting at your feet.

It was the river. Far away and late
I heard the story of the overturned canoe,
your call, "go help the others," and the great heart stayed
in death. Think of that country that we knew
so well, land of black woods and trailing vines
and inland muddy streams that held your fate,
the Pollywogs, the flooded Danville mines,
Sangamon and Vermilion and Salt Fork,
our professorial playground. How we played
beside the crawfish-catfish-haunted Lethe stream
through overall-and-gallus groves of Academe.
Sulphured for chiggers, through the green opaque
fills of the scoops we swam, and dried in air,
played softball in cow-pastures, fried our steak,
stood by the fire and rocked the night with corny song
and shone the moon with outlaw rye and legal beer.
And now you are gone out of a world gone wrong.
Spirit is storm. You can not catch and keep it near.
Verse will not hold you fixed. The river took
you, and your spirit on the plains
will shout with the old laughter over all my pains
to put a man alive inside a book.
End from an epitaph you turned me to:
the tribute to a Roman Spanish charioteer:
*Now pour the wine. Your friends and flowers are here.*
*Never forget. For there was none like you.*

[163]

## DRAMATIS PERSONAE

Wardrobes of empty doublets stalk the stage.
My chorus gathers wool and mutters what
is more like me than sense. The sad kings rage
and die their destinies. How do I rig
my thoughts to yours? We sew them in a knot
of noise and hooks of lines. Before the cardboard scene
the patterns of convention, the coiffed queen,
forever one-eyed knave, and frosty king of hearts
act their foreseen and necessary parts
to beat your nerves and eyes with what has never been.
How was the lie so tragic and so big?
The princess grieved for love and shook her hair.
Nothing inside. She spoke of passion so.
That lovely head was spouting from wild air.

*[164]*

# RETURN TO THE CASTELLI

On Monte Cavo a bulb of defense has sprouted. It masters
the mirror of the forest girl, the kingly branch and the oak leaves,
the pope's castle that was a hood of blessing above the waters.

We mooned on up as when we were young, Frascati to Tusculum.
Boy scouts in paper shields and swords of wood were enacting
games of Roman against Latin, very seriously

squatting in the ditch of the Cyclopean, the prehistoric
road to ambuscade the enemy. It was a feast day.
The Lambretta lover and his pillion lass were there in the bushes.

We strolled and stopped in the sacred forest once of our courting
days. Issuing late Latin winter sun warmed the strings
of knees and articulated the precise progress of ankles.

We sat for too-new wine in a forest of vats hogsheads
and spigots, giggling at each other across the greenish
stuff in the tumblers, silly as a couple of adolescents.

Memory becalms us, it shines. But in the green of our ice
there is a fly stuck. We can't get at it to take it out.
Pretend it isn't there and continue in hours translucent.

We inhabit a world jammed with old hates, black wrongs. The frame twists.
Monkeys men and mice are getting thrown at the moon and the planets.
What end who knows. We go on with our mature occupations.

Some middle hours of this life are lazy and blond as honey.

*[165]*

## FERRY JUNCTION

The old bus rattled downhill and stopped at the jetty. We got out.
Piles floated beards of moss in thick water. Holes
showed in the landing boards. Always we were docile. We stood there

in line at a table where the old man was sitting.
A brass stud fastened the soiled shirt over his adam's apple
and the silver bristles on his neck. With the stub of a pencil

he wrote our tickets one by one, painfully inserting
two carbons for three sheets apiece. It took half an hour.
Our careful feet rocked the boat as we stepped down on thwarts.

And it was too full of course. The motor stalled three times going
over. We all stood and smoked. It was too dark to see much.
(They had told us the boat and water would be full of brides

and babies, young men lost in battle, the wreckage of youth
and dreams and tears, glories foregone, bright loves forgotten.)
A rat's head ran out a slim wake that pittered

and plinked on the stones. Gray grew in that light the lilies
beyond the margin. Then in black water arms, hips, elbows
stirred, fattened to white, turned over and sank, as the keel slid

soft over flesh. Some hair, I think, streamed on that surface.
At the far side a few piles and planks were sketched. Here
as we lurched ashore one by one the grubby old hand

accepted, once now and forever, the shabby stubs of our tickets.

*[166]*

# SESTINA FOR A FAR-OFF SUMMER

We cradled the heavy green canoe in our arms
and walked it down the steep path to the river.
To launch and land the weight was all our problem.
We stormed the current (how the arms of youth
are strong) and found our beach below the forest
golden in early afternoon of summer.

That was the careless story of all our summer.
Sun was warm gold and water sweet on arms.
We changed and dried behind the ferns in the forest.
Our private sandy beach far up the river
was bright with laughter, blond-and-white with youth
and looks. Our innocence found there no problem

of sweet complicity. The only problem
was how to hold all through one golden summer
the careless posture of our temperate youth.
All our embrace was water in our arms.
Our only summer love was our cold river.
Here lay the fond adventure of the forest.

Our river wore the green sleeves of the forest
that spelled on her slow depth the mirrored problem
of dark green trees reversed upon the river.
We skimmed the calm with flat stones, all that summer,
slung from the sinewy whip of our thin arms.
To carve water was all desire of our youth.

In time of sunset air and the first youth
of evening, shore fires burned before the forest
and all its gloom behind. The bending arms
of swimmers made their rippled wakes a problem
of crossing lines on that midnight midsummer
black-and-gold slippery surface of the river.

And summertime comes back and means the river
and irresponsible grace and careless youth
when we were young and wasted all our summer
and would not see the world beyond the forest,
the adult life to win, the task, the problem,
the angry nations and the globe in arms.

Leave us our time of the river, our time of forest
and green of youth when the world was still no problem
since all that summer we held the world in our arms.

*[168]*

# THE STRIDE OF TIME

THE SKELETON IN THE CLOSET

Mr Jeremy Bentham sits, nearly complete,
inside a booth in the University College hall,
a skeleton, decently dressed in neat
sad clothes: all
but his head. That lies, boiled, in a box at his feet.

Thus, on those occasions
when the closet, labeled JEREMY BENTHAM, is laid
open to view, while preparations
for a directors' meeting are made,
a head of wax stares down our grisliest patience.

Jeremy's bones wear the neat
costume; since he was dissected
in the presence of his friends, and all meat
removed: so he directed.
Now his bones sit with the academic elite.

Pedestrian, utilitarian, debonair,
dreamless, dispassionately kind,
his logic is philosophy's despair.
It cracks the metaphysics of the mind.
The system crumbles, but the sense is there.

[169]

But if so, what sense
dedicated his bones to play this part
in the teeth of omnivorous immense
death? A contemptuous or clinging human heart?
Be that as it may. At all events,

when the last angels bugle, from their stones
and holes, all such fossils, scraps of shell,
hair-hanks, forlorn bits of skeletons
as comprise us, you will be most ready to answer the bell,
Mr. Bones.

[170]

## COLOSSUS ASTRIDE

Lost my way,
summer's hottest day,
in grass brown as hay

on hill-bones aswarm
with grasshoppers, warm
brown spry uniform

and crazy, all
joints, stems, and vertical
elbows, vul-

nerable and in my
power. Giant I
tower, too high

to see, too grand to know.
They feel me there, though;
frantically say so.

Murder, if the brute
lets one monstrous foot
stamp its boot.

If I could climb
out, there'd be a little time
for peace. I'm

all the God they can
know, a tall foolish man
with no plan.

[171]

# WABASH BLUES

## 1

Once to this privacy of tree and town
I came, conquest in blood and flush on finger pad
for glory, and contact here grew sad and failed.
Nails' end, my spells fused out, and stunned
      my arm.
I could not gather light on maples, pinch
and nerve a wood, glove down my hands
      in gloom
of shrubs scapeless from clasp. They would
      not stay.
How make a copse of druids come alive?
Single in lone brown castles, baron of rush-
lit vacancies, that winter fingered out
its hours in joints of twigs brittle and broken
over wires.
      How did it go?
            Now June
is full of windows and calls back the runes
in coils of rivers grooved as deep as hills.
How green that glory grown, so once unseen.

## 2

Alone in my upstairs room in the D.A.R. house,
with a skinny rug on the floor, a reading lamp
      in a steel shade,
a dozen books and two chairs, I called it
      my castle,
dead center, dead bull's eye, innermost
      ingrowth, but I dreamed
escape lines. Here Monon and Big Four cross.
      Flat northward
a queen of cities dabbled slattern toes in her
      own unsalted
pale sea. Down south, drawled the neverseen
      imagined honeyland.

West the rails fled back with my thoughts past
       the Veedersburg corn-tower,
but east oh east lay future, the Bremen
       gleaming up the northern
circle, breaching the salt castles. But why
       so much elsewhere
than is, and the queens near, the gardens
       over the fence grow
as elsewhere lilies, green grow the forests
       near in Brown County
and close overdrape these Hoosier rivers.
       What then did I
do with all my chambers and beds of leisure
       but toss and imagine
me far, homesick, lovesick, salt-and-spray
       nostalgic?
You and I, two squares in the same wrong hole,
       Ezra. Remember?

     3

Heart's winter. Sat it through.
In his maple-grown mansion up the street
Lew Wallace drew
the blinds, and dreamed out his complete

phony world. Alone
in a growth of face, fact,
and frame, our false stone
castles cracked

and windows fell apart.
Dilapidation. All
here denied the green heart;
and the atom swirl and fall

of live faces passed us by.
Stupid Lew. Stupid I.

## WITNESS TO DEATH

Disconsolate I
from the thinning line
have seen friends drop and die.
All I called mine
has gone or will go
from its place in the sun.
This we know,
and nothing can be done.

Villon, Nashe, Dunbar,
to your great testaments
I too assent from afar,
bestow my violence,
and throw my rhyme
and rage in the feeding face
of the great pig of time.
Beauty gone from her place

wit wasted and lost,
promise killed with blight,
McCarter and George Frost,
Dilys who was delight,
Gilly suddenly gone,
Cartwright killed in the air,
Forrester, Conklin undone
in their prime. Where, where

is the rose, and the great
heart, and the shine of wit?
I hate death. I hate
all who speak well of it.
Dunbar, Nashe, Villon,
we sang as best we could
for the sake of those who are gone,
and it does no good.

*[174]*

# CLAUDIA GOODBYE

*(From a Roman Epitaph)*

Claudia the Roman hailed us from her grave.
Stand, stranger, friend, and read me. What I say
is not much. Pride shortens words to the way-
farer's haste, the desperate "traveler, stay"
is said with dignity. Remember me.
The tomb is nothing. I was beautiful.
Or it's the stone that spoke in letters. She
was lovely, not the monument, to see.
Claudia was the name her parents gave.
She loved her husband in her heart, it says,
deilexit, diligently, with delight
or what? And from such loving nights and days
together, she gave birth
to two sons, one of whom she left on earth
and one beneath it when she lost her light
(Cornelia with one dead jewel now).
Read on. Pleasant to talk to, and her step was neat.
Did I not tell you she was beautiful?
She was a housekeeper. She worked in wool.
And that is all, for I have spoken. Go.
She lives in letters, and the gravestone's art
pins down forever one time out of time,
and stops the squeeze of death that stopped the heart
so long as the eyes read, and the words chime,
and the brain loves the shape behind the rhyme,
and Psyche stirs in the embrace of butterflies
and eyes that were her eyes and are my eyes.

So, Claudia. And have you told us all?
You speak so well, and can you not recall
just some unlicensed moment from behind the grave?

[175]

We ask no confidence, but was there not some incomplete
time, sense of failure, moments not so neat
to gather to your basket, when that precious wool
was dead in the fingers, and the mind gone dull
and stale with ease and trying to contrive
some fact to want and want and not to have,
and the desire to want lost in the course
of state and matron's honors and the full
long dutiful and dedicated hours?
Speak, Claudia, speak.

                  But I have spoken. Call
no more.
            But was this all? Claudia, all?


I speak for her. I am the gravestone. I
tell you, good friend, in Claudia's name, goodbye.
Now give her leave to say: Leave me alone.
Your Claudia is written on the stone
for you to read. The rest is Claudia's own.

*[176]*

# THE PHI BETA KAPPA POEM

*William and Mary College, 1961*

You are elect and young,
and grown to bright new honors in a place
ancient for courtesy and wit. I wish my song
could only have hailed your state, with hope and grace.
But here, in our corner of a universe gone wrong,

even the metaphysical man
finds his brains running out of his ears,
clutches for quicksilver moments where he can
between the seizures of his self-grown fears,
and finds a wall to huddle from the hurricane.

And as this ship of fools yaws extravagantly
blown at adventure, cracked against the blind
wrong strong battering brute of a sea,
what barely tolerable course is there to find,
what other steersman than Philosophy,

old, stubborn, hard of hearing, cross
and discredited though he be? To you,
a young, nameless, numbered, living piece
of the world's intelligence come true,
I would say: Live as you are made, count no loss

neighbor to defeat, so long as your kind
shines out of the black cave. Never despair.
Live down the prophets. While still the mind
moves in its starry course, the keys are there,
and the way up to the light still there for you to find.

*[177]*

# DRUNKEN OLD SOLIPSISTS IN A BAR

In their own cool gray alcoholic world
sealed from the sun at any time of day,
you find this circle of old heads. A glass
that fills and drains and fills again with gold
sits before each, to tranquilize the spirit
and burn slow fires in the stupescent brain.

The gray bar is the inside of a brain
selfgrown and shuttered on the outward world,
where, clammed in its own fumy smell, the spirit
rapt in the microcosm of its day
spells out the cloistered hours and guzzles gold
from the inverted barrel of the glass;

as if, gray in a cave or belled in glass,
this bar, the unique inside of the brain,
trimmed with brown wood and bottles painted gold,
subsisted as the all and only world,
with no outside, no windows, and no day,
its walls, all body grown upon the spirit;

and there, reliving glory in strong spirits
as in the flattery of a magic glass,
they know themselves as on a younger day
with April lyrics singing in the brain,
the past recaptured to a rainbow world
drenched in fond sunshine and philosopher's gold.

The catfoot barkeep doles his bottled gold,
and television, ectoplasmic spirit,
gray-glimmering ghost of the external world,
gibbers and mimes behind its convex glass,

with incantations feeds and stills the brain
on distillations filmed from the live day.

Then doors open, and into dazzling day
of summer afternoon with all its gold,
old knees, jerked by the strings of a half-blind brain,
float them toward home like disembodied spirits,
with faces stuffed and set, and eyes like glass,
and one still grin to give to all the world.

All through the drunken day this larval spirit
builds his bright palaces of gold and glass
in the domed brain which forms his private world.

*[179]*

## IKON FOR A FALL-OUT SHELTER

*(From a painting by Fritz Janschka)*

Against a Götterdämmerung glow,
angels bending, white and gold, with the frown
of furious children, all in a row
hack at and try to beat down

something. What? We shall have time to kill,
and a conversation piece will go far
here, where we take our lasting seats and fill
the lethal chamber whose white rats we are.

So, while our world ends in the street
outside, we can sit still and contemplate
angels with axe and halberd stooping to beat
down human idiocy that has no shape

of dragon cockatrice or ape
to hurt and hate.

[180]

CATANIA TO ROME

The later the train was at every station,
the more people were waiting to get on,
and the fuller the train got, the more time it lost,

and the slower it went, all night, station to station,
the more people were on it, and the more people
were on it, the more people wanted to get on it,

waiting at every twilight midnight and half-daylight
station, crouched like runners, with a big suitcase
in each hand, and the corridor was all elbows armpits

knees and hams, permessos and per favores, and a suitcase
always blocking half the corridor, and the next station
nobody got off but a great many came aboard.

When we came to our station we had to fight to get off.

[181]

SOUVENIRS OF SICILY

The crumbled busts asleep in the noon noise,
the cape of masonry from a lost day
pointing into south wind and soft blue miles,
the disemboweled shark in the bright bay,
the tall girl with the long beer-colored hair
laughing alone among her crowd of boys,
and, flirting by the gateway to the school,
young girls in black and blonde seraphic smiles,
papyrus strict as Egypt in the pool
distilled from springs too deep and cold to know,
the broken house with garbage on the floor.
The garden of the mind combines it so,
but if we go back, will all still be there?
Such flowers grow in the filth along that shore.

[182]

## CARTESIAN MOMENTS

How shall I know the world, or even see
dimension dreaming in a plain of tiles,
when all the scene is papered out and thinned
to surface without essence, and flat miles?
What population makes a world of things
outside this empty universe of me?
From my false belvedere and balcony,
hats and umbrellas in the street below
could be beetles, or platters moved on springs.
These are God's metaphors, for all I know,
stuck on the pane of this unwindowed eye,
with no more depth to take their inwards by
than silly mobiles clanking in the wind.
Who in this lonely world but only I?

[183]

# NIGHT-BLOOMING ROSES

Branching they grew
faces glimpsed on the garden
wall, lived and knew
well the warden
of their shape, till one, true

to future, dared unsheathe
from thorn and leaf, came,
arms full of clothes, to breathe
and be in the cham-
ber, sleep beneath

sheets, and go away
after hours. Such brushed beauties walk
sleep. After love, they
grow back on the stalk
and fade for day.

*[184]*

# EAGLE OVER THE COAST

*(In memory of Robinson Jeffers)*

Bigger than us rest. All's now written.
The lines stride in, hump to angles, smitten
bleed gray at the edge and smash; wake
the demon in skull's keep and brain's cowl, make
tower's kingdom, wolf's king, for claw
pelt and rut-reek time's apostle, law
of giant club and dog against the bull,
zodiac's black and gold, memory of polar frost
before mankind, seismic spasm and slabbed coast
upshuddered. Your blood's tides to beck of moon pull
shrink and flood; but, sprung from tempest, you rise, rise
to steep and air, dwindle on wings, harry
high birds, drop the world, and marry
space. Since Hardy, no such eagle sailed our skies.

*[185]*

# LATE ALONE

Once more, my dear,
I keep the solitaire: the glass,
cigarette, memory of elsewhere blear
my wake-hours that I grin at as I pass.
I wish you were here.

All comfort dies.
The screen is only me and me is thin.
The love-shapes group and pose behind my eyes
and look like you. No substance is within
to materialize.

At two o'clock
the mockingbirds churrow and jeer
at false dawn. Mockingbirds mock.
I pity me because you are not here.
I hold and rock

my old brave
ego, all that I have to take to bed.
It is a fragment without you to rest above.
The love-shape mocks me from inside my head.
Good night, my love.

*[186]*

## SKY DIVING

They step from the high plane and begin to tumble
down. Below is the painted ground, above
is bare sky. They do not fumble
with the catch, but only fall; drop sheer; begin to move

in the breakless void; stretch and turn, freed
from pressure; stand in weightless air
and softly walk across their own speed;
gather and group, these dropping bundles, where

the neighbor in the sky stands, reach touch
and clasp hands, separate and swim
back to station (did swimmer ever shear such
thin water?) falling still. Now at last pull the slim

cord. Parasols bloom in the air, slow
the swift sky-fall. Collapsed tents cover
the ground. They rise up, plain people now.
Their little sky-time is over.

*[187]*

# YANNINA AND ALI PASHA

I will go hide
in a monastery lost
in an island, with my bride.
No man shall know that unknown coast,
nor land and break inside.

What can be more hidden
than an island in a lake, reed
guarded, face averted, ridden
to in boats, and at need
pulled in on itself, to fend the unbidden?

Ali Pasha, he
of the broad chest and Turkish beard,
lord of the north in strong suzerainty,
bloody-handed, Greek-feared,
took the Christian, Kyra Basilike

to be his bride
(we let strangers in) but rode the land
hard. Souliote women walked off the cliff and died
to beat the chase and the red hand.
From the castle's dungeon on the other side

Kyra Phrosyne, bound
by Ali's moustachioed bravoes, gagged,
thrown from a boat and drowned
in clear clean depths none dragged
for her poor rotting beauty, and none found

afterward, speaks
from large scared eyes. Turn beneath the mosque, take
the shabbier way. The slaughterhouse leaks
its gutterful of blood into the lake.
Under the calm front history reeks.

At last Ali fled
to the island sanctuary in the trees.
The assassins came and hacked him in his bed,
and beautiful Kyra Basilike's
pillowy bosom propped his dying head.

Yannina, green
in spring for willows, soft for lake air,
beneath the filigree silver screen
of art, the broken ribs lie bare,
and the torn vitals bleed between.

And where the tall
minaret and the mosque, Bohemund's dungeon-keep,
and the dilapidated castle wall
tied together with ivy, sleep,
Ali, in their sleep they remember all.

How could this dreamy lake
town, this waterland soft as a fish, then
in the treason of its bland embrace take
Basilike, Phrosyne, and their men,
and cause the heart of the north to break?

## SONNET ON HOPE

Bedraggled daughter of Desire and Fear,
she'll glaze your eyes and sing your brain to sleep,
pour siren's wax and honey in your ear.
Hope, self-seduced and simple, counting her sheep.
The painted Hope, blind, whispering, and with wings.
The baby-sitter in the abandoned chair
waiting beside a phone that never rings,
dreaming of cradles and fixed calendars,
and the clock stopped forever, and the glass
sucking its sand back in, the never-was
world come again, new-made and clean of scars.
I fled from Hope and found her everywhere,
barefoot and bold in all her slattern charms,
with a two-headed baby in her arms.

*[190]*

# SESTINA OF SANDBARS AND SHELTERS

Here on the sandbar in a circle of friends
we lie at ease under the striped shelter
and watch the haze and water light a world
of chairs and children all a summertime
long afternoon before the light is gone.
The time, late summer, and the year is now.

O sky and sand and blue of here and now,
how shall we keep you always for our friends
and us, and for our sons when we are gone,
or save some certainty for all, and shelter
the dream of living for a piece of time
within a known and tolerable world?

This could be the last summer for the world.
The rat race into doom is running now,
and none can win the race run against time.
Where is our help? We cannot trust our friends,
and God our hope holds out no visible shelter
from this stormblast. Perhaps our chance is gone.

The days of Noah and his ark are gone
when he escaped out of a drowning world
and held selected life inside the shelter
of that strong hull. How shall we shelter now
inside a world of fable and make friends
with simple beasts, and save some seed for time?

And still we walk as if we still had time
on our long sandbar till the light is gone,
sit in the boathouse and are gay with friends,

talk shop and sports and reassess the world
of art, as if in time just after now
the race would wait and we could find some shelter

other than that evil gray squat ashbrick shelter
that waits on every corner for the time
when the blast is no longer next but now,
the switch pulled and all chance to stop it gone,
where in the holocaust of the human world
we crowd inside and shoot our clamoring friends.

What shelter until the day has come and gone
is found in this sick time that blights the world
where all are enemies now and hate their friends?

*[192]*

# MONASTERY ON ATHOS

*(From a poster)*

Rock wrinkles, folds on the near
face, but profiles to sheer

fall. From rock grows four-
square the essential core

as near white as pale
butter. Horizontal frail

balconies project on hatched
timbers, angled like eyelashes, matched

to their own shadow. Outer roofs slant gray
enclosing the chapel dome, gay

scarlet over white. Lower foreground
one sloping half drowned

rock creams the incumbent sea's
blue mass. One gull wings his vees

to cross where the lower cliff slants
the line. One sailship breaks the long expanse

of blue. Above, beyond, brown shore is lowerlined by
white, leaving only paler sky

where for upper right corner one white puff
of cloud is enough

to compose color mass and steer the eye
as gull ship and I

wheel by and admire the Byzantine
monastery scene.

[193]

GAME RESUMED

My locker, green steel,
hung on its hooks a row
of old shorts and T-
shirts, sneakers down at the heel
I wore eight years ago,
still there waiting for me.

Rectangular pit, white
walls flooded in light
are still and always the same.
Why did I ever let go?
Old men can play this game.
Legs slow,
eyes unsharpen, but the wrist
still drives the shape of play,
where the antagonist
is partner. Fadeaway
backhand to front wall
drops softly into place,
as turn by turn we chase
the black sinewy ball,
and, by twos and fours, our deep
drives and corner slants
weave the pattern we keep
turn by turn like a dance.

So, after half an hour,
and after eight years or more
elapsed, after the shower,
we are what we have been,
back where we were before
on the bench at the green
and steel locker, on whose wall
the shorts and the outworn ball
on the corner of the shelf
held, these years between
(forgotten and unseen),
my self.

EX-U.S. 40

The town sits forsaken up on the hill.
Once the post road went through.
The shell of a Greyhound Station is still
there. Three houses are new,

but empty lots fester with trash. The church
is overgrown and the bandstand rotted away.
Seven ladies are sitting on the porch,
drinking iced tea in the heat of the late day

and not minding it. The new road far below
hums with contemporary cars
along its stylish curves, and does not know
its past in the fragments of old scars

branching off. Let the old growth sicken on its hill.
But somewhere in our forgotten corners, see
the comfortable ladies sitting still
on the porch, drinking their cold tea.

[195]

VERSE

Nothing sacred here: no hysterical woman chewing
buckthorn: no bardic beard on the high hill line communing
with stars and muses: not the sea-wood groaning in wild weather:

not (always) oil or endless waters welling up, caught and
channeled: nor yet the lapidary's chisel pecking
limited stone: it is not salting a walk of pebbles

or sea shells, or draping driftwood in weed: still less is it
to open the abdominal wall and invite approval
of my intestines displayed: it is not confessional:

but comes of some oyster's-irritant, some cinder promoting
iris and spangle: that will not tolerate tranquility, until the
percept is caught, sealed, fused, transposed as artifact.

The process itself is too undignified to be worth description.

*[196]*

## OF SEVEN SINS

### Sloth

Raptured and fat with sleep, I watch the day
grow old for hours in windows. Now I rise
and doze the rest. The animus behind my eyes,
so tired, strands on a marge of broken sleep
and tells its idiot numbers, counts its sheep
in day stupors to fudge the hours away.
I read the book I read three times before
or sit and glare along the floor.
I am the clover field where summer hums
all day in wings of other bees than I,
the mail box where the postman never comes,
the blues singer too weary to be blue,
the pig enchanted in his golden sty.
My dearest vice. Siren stuff. I love you.

### Pride

Not combs and mirrors, glory in shape and hair
displayed, seen. Not peacocks on the grass,
mermaids in shallows. Pride's not anywhere
but in the word, to comprise and compass
the unseen arrogance that sets me free
to measure man by me.
Not looks nor dress. Pride will not shine
in sense, that's vanity. Pride is the voice
of my recoiling will that knots its choice,
and no one's voice but mine,
but my voice that says always me, not you,
that all must be unseen, unless I see,
but my voice, that says no truth can be true
as any untruth that shows true to me.

[197]

*Anger*

Think of lions and martyrs, gas chamber, condemned cell.
We cast back into self and know too well
who sleeps here after sessions in this cold hell.

Gauleiters and gallows, Chessman, Eichmann keep
us company by night and populate the sleep
of eyes too worn and washed to weep

for Socrates and Christ and Jezebel.
So did we hang the shepherd or his lost sheep?
No man is free. Some spent fires smell.


*Avarice*

Danaë in her shower, and the stuff drifting down
by cracks and corners, day long, she's washed, rolled,
lapped in persistent and affectionate gold.
Are dolls in attics bait to frail divinity?
What's she to me, except to call my own,
clasp, sequester, hold close, keep
warm and store beneath my pillow when I sleep?
I am no prince who loiters a romantic wood.
This dreaming girl is called security.
I'm more wizard. I'd trap the sun if I could,
but want it solid, cannot fumble or see
credit, but like a peasant with his buried sock
I keep my Danaë behind a golden lock
turned with a golden key.

[198]

*Envy*

So, hate my neighbor. Wisdom, stature
elsewhere define
the form of man nature
never made mine.
Or it shall be, if once mine,
never again.
I see it shine
in other men.
I cannot surpass it
nor yet ignore it.
My neighbor has it.
Hate him for it.


*Lust*

Boys in the plaza watching the girls go by.
The old goat with the glad and gooey eye.
The sailor homing back to Circe's sty.

Looking. Action undoes. Making in mind
takes such possession of our womankind.
Who could love thus, being blind?

Strapped on, self-masted, how we look and move
and sail in naked memories, prove
the abject pastime that beguiles our love.

[199]

*And Gluttony*

They use a pig to chase truffles. He noses out
the smell, black and lovely, begins to root,
and is whacked smartly on the snout.
The truffle becomes a grail, an absolute,
a perfection passing pigliness. Now the pig
eats no truffles, but learns to stand still
and point like a hound. In a world too big
for this pig, I take it ill
that our love for a truffle is a love none can fulfill.

*[200]*

# LORD BOUNTIFUL'S RAID

They flew very high, and over the target unloaded
their cargo, so that the North China sky
on that bright noon positively exploded
an assault of goodies, dropping from on high
canned Hormel hams, evaporated milk,
California sherry, sides of frozen beef,
each to its parachute of straining silk,
Old Overholt and cheeses, beyond belief
commingled in descent, and far below
on Tientsin flats the villagers ran out
in wonderment that we could use them so,
to stare, gesticulate, and point and shout,
and report to the bewildered commissars
they were invaded from a sky gone mad
with supermarkets dropping from the stars
their precious hoards, and still the heavens rained
potato chips in drums, jam in glass jars,
whole pineapples, and tiny cans of strained
baby food, and cases of candy bars.

*[201]*

# MY UNCLE

I think of forests palaces and swans
and Chinese painted scrolls and figured silk,
breakfasts of wine-and-tapioca soup,

of limericks and psalms, jade rings and beer,
of mad King Ludwig on his porcelain eggs,
a baroque cardinal or the knave of clubs.

An elder. So much younger when he died
than I am now. Blood bursting in the head.
Florence, which he loved best who holds him now.

Once slim, they tell me, so poetical.
I knew a leisured height, a handsome head,
bold nose, a ripe mouth, and fastidious hands.

He would amuse spoiled children. Catholic
spellbound childlike in ceremony. What
hard faith stuck underneath, this puzzles me.

His mind as a cathedral arched and domed.
Musing imagination flew such form
as could not think to lose all opulence.

Rococo is the word. A glory grew
exotic to its circumstance, so loved,
smiled on, encouraged, and misunderstood.

Dreamy my uncle drifts on pinkish clouds.
His heaven or my hope, how shall I know?
His cherubs would sing well. I hope they do.

*[202]*

# A MEDITATION FOR SAINT LUCY'S DAY

The electric grate burns simulated coals. Day's down
to a filler shining between broad layers of black.
My system mutters outrage. But I think of Saint Lucy,

the blonde girl from Italy walking through the night in Sweden
knocking on door after door, admitted, her head radiant
with candles; then coffee and cake given, house after house

shining and singing in the dark Santa Lucia. A martyr.
Is it no more than that elderly gallants must court their Persephones
by rape and death ravishing the flower gatherers in the meadows?

Or no more than sad wish? Chauncey Depew sat next Mary Garden,
she in a strapless dress, Mary my dear, what holds that thing up?
Your age, Mr. Depew, your age. Or Mr. Justice

Holmes, and the pretty girl passing by, and oh
to be seventy again. Such ways, deep weather, heart starves for summer,
cuddling material innocence in the elderly dark.

But that's the old solitary confinement, the solipsist hammering
on his last walls. I would be with others in the lighted
room, clutching a little coffee, tobacco and cake

and candles comfort and Lucy against the surrounding solstice.

*[203]*

## BEGIN AUTUMN HERE

Unbuild the form of heat upon
the scattered and displayed shapes of slate
water. Here the half-sunken stone
sharpens its mirror to cold silence; pines wait

wind's collapse to sheathe them in no sound;
stars cool in night water. Here
build, too, illusion. This stone-and-root-cross-writhen ground
grows bone and nerve, decays. The bold hemisphere

faces harsh dynasty. Angry suns glare
and wheel back, and night blanks. Even we
clutter the springs of our outriding air
with our bad wisdom and brainfall of debris.

Our world will wreck on despair yet. Still
water will slate, stone shine, star
drown, Illusion is as real as real.
Imagination is what we are.

*[204]*

# SCENE FROM THE WORKING CLASS

*To Richard Hoggart*

Two nasty little houses back to back.
The single room smelling of sister's face
powder and father's tripe-and-onion stew,
the coin box full of pennies on the shelf
and all a family's future held in place.
Each week was like each week. This was your self
and father come in late from mill or mine
and Mondays mother hung the washing on the line.
Sunday sacred to the last generation,
uncle and aunt, grandparents coming in
to tea. You always opened up a tin
of pineapple and one of salmon. Celebration.
Two nasty little houses back to back,
and one held you and all your family,
your coal fire company savings love and heat,
your girl and future wife from down the street,
and when the poker banged against the grate
behind the wall, it meant a heart attack
or baby's coming, and you could not wait.

*[205]*

## SCÈNE DE LA VIE ANTÉRIEURE

By corners splashed in sun for afternoon,
and most by night's long memory, through the town
and out the long streets striding he goes by,
a clothes-pin like a man, with a rag
of silk pinched in his arm, flapped like a flag;
scarecrow or frightened crow he seems to be,
saying, as you are now so once was I,
and what I am now ye shall be.
Brain in its bone-hood ticks in the drizzle, dry
in the mist, he cannot even sort his husks
or deal the bones on the board, he is too thin.
He cannot open and let the water in.
Crows wheel his square, infest his towers.
Saying, there are my darlings all asleep,
and saying, some must lie too cold to keep,
wear angels carved with smiles above their bones.
Why can they not come back? Saying, I dare
anything now. It is no longer worst to die.
The worst is not to care.
Indifference is made immortal in the bone
and damned to feel for feeling.
                                    For next year
the shy and secret future buds are here,
and green and here the coming spring is grown.
The buds walk hand in hand and eye to eye.
Flapping his black among them he goes by,
saying, where are my ghosts, do I still care?
Saying, what I am now, you too shall be,
as you are now so once was I;
saying, your crows will come; remember me.

[206]

## THE STICKS

By Lake Averno a boy squatted in the trash heap picking
in the broken glass and tin cans, crying hey, you speak
English you speak English hey? And the most about the lake water

was it looked dirty. Giving up, recovering the shed of a railway
station with a dripping latrine I took the next train back
to the city. Is it not truly wonderful to be able to slink

away from drizzle and ditch, to feed warm and pamper
this sack of senses, me? Have I not that whoremaster imagination
to beguile me with paradise and flower girls and the illusion

of escape from the terminal and poisoned shore? Which yet I have seen.
The other side of the river. The dump. The boneyard. Where
the incinerator lives. The compost heap. Where all are awaited

by the idiot who mumbles as he picks at the trash he is lord of.

[207]

## OLD HEMINGWAY

Looking at last from his purgatorio
and what imagined growing out of the mind's
mist and the alcohol: a stony hillside
and asphodel waving its strengthless heads
above dry grasshoppers as perished souls
of warriors once as angular as they:
or wards of beds for old men, where the nurse
chatters and plumps the pillows, and orderly
subfiends in white dish out the daily cigarette,
the weekly sherry or the annual girl:
rations are purgatory, and he dreams
forward or is it back to paradise
and the wave dimpled at the Cyprian feet:
he lost his world of servants in white coats,
comic headwaiters thought as wise as kings
serving him Capri Scala chilled in pails
to warm the mistress never found as wives,
his childish nymph who so admired old satyrs
or old counts or colonels, old writers past writing:
but more he lost, the painter's hand in the stroke
that drew the gray taste of coffee, at iron
tables set next the street and by string chairs,
the sidewalk look, light growing in whose trees
washed last night's conscience from the shabby teeth:
drew duck on tarns and windows full of fish
or war's look sprawled as soldiers all asleep
in the corridor and one who sat to watch
block stations and canals go by the window
and the hours clicking out on joints of rails:
lost youth lost art and mumbled till he knew
he mumbled, and so drew the trigger: like one
of his own brave decrepit fighters dancing
his final grace of now uncertain art
too close against the horns, which speared him home.

*[208]*

## DOLPHIN SEEN ALONE

One dolphin.
                    Strongly curved, watertight
and snug, zippered in
to suit of dark green skin
he sprouts and plunges. Bulk and blunt snout bite
gunmetal gray water, and no land's in sight.

Our kith and kin.
Like us, carries in his skin
branched blood and red muscle. Lives with fish
but breathes air. Can smile talk wish.
Bores green depth by strength and speed
not as ours. All we need
he does not need.

This one's almost,
if a dolphin could be, lost,
lone in a huge sea, where no sea girl pillion-rides
his dark green sides,
conveys no poet to the shore beyond sight.
Alone, sullen or thoughtful. Bulk and snout bite
out dull curves of flight.

Who would not want to be
a dolphin, fold into great green gray sea
like a dolphin thinking out
with trim bulk and blunt snout
the curve and plunge of everlasting flight?

*[209]*

## THE SESTINA AFTER DANTE

Within the grove that keeps its cup of shade
in the small valley set between the hills,
as in a chapel roofed with leaves, and grass
upon the floor, and chastely dressed in green,
all to herself and on a chair of stone,
we have enshrined the idea of a lady

which is projected from our living lady,
formed from her change of moods in light and shade
of her still grace as sculptured out of stone;
and we have climbed these hot and mortal hills
to find her always in a shower of green
leaf-light, presiding on our private grass.

As fresh as dew that strings the morning grass,
the airs and looks that grow upon this lady
are like light caught in groves forever green,
remote as years gone by, and cool as shade
in summer, or as wind among the hills,
or clear spring water running over stone.

And for all time as quiet as a stone
we could sit by her feet upon the grass
in the small valley set between the hills.
Simply to look and idolize this lady
is to forget the stride of time, the shade
of night, and that no branch is always green,

that autumn comes to crisp and brown our green
grace, and enchant our vigors into stone,
as the tall trees advance their shape of shade
to darken all the color of the grass
and close the farewell outline of our lady
as the last light goes out behind the hills,

and we walk down among the barren hills,
blanched with the blight upon our hope, and green
with fear, to that sad place where Pluto's lady
Persephone, with face and heart of stone,
broods over asphodel and withered grass;
there flitter with the rest, a perished shade.

We'll sleep in little hills and under stone
and the long grass upon these graves be green,
mourned by our lady in the cypress shade.

*[211]*

BATHTUBS

Scoops in the sea rock full of natural water,
used petrol drums, old oaken buckets oversized,
glossy ceramics, thermal springs, pot holes,

anything serves: the Soochow tub, majestic,
fed with hot pitchers; Scythian, steamed in mist
of hemp; the social clusters of the Japanese.

Have cargoes. Thoughtful omphalopsychite.
The athlete's sluice of sweat. The foreman's Saturday night.
A siren leers through the conniving foam,

advertising come-hither or soaps for sale.
Kings come to it, or in the Mycenaean
asaminthys, Homer's heroes scrubbed by queens.

I had for boat once an old brown tin bathtub
tabbed with twin ears for soap and plugged with a cork,
and sailed on a small pond until it drowned.

The Three of Gotham used, I think, a bathtub.
Poppaea brimmed her tub with donkey's milk.
Lady Godiva mistook one for a horse.

My dreamboats sail by night such perilous seas.
In the middle of the salon and the dressed people
I in my bathtub, dreading I may be noticed.

Better I like, above the dwindling earth,
to fly my hip-winged old flat-bottomed bathtub
through slippery space, and past the floating stars.

[212]

# A STRICT LADY STRICTLY GUARDED

*(The Sestina of Arnaut Daniel)*

The firm will which in my heart enters
cannot be torn away by beak nor nail
of the flatterer who swears away his soul.
Since I dare not beat him down with branch nor switch,
so then by fraud, where there forbids no uncle,
I'll take my joy, in orchard or in room.

And when I think upon that room
where to my cost I know no man may enter,
where all's more strict with me than brother or uncle,
no part of me but trembles, even the nail,
as trembles the small child before the switch,
such fear I have, and too much for my soul.

So for the body, not the soul,
may she consent to see me in her room.
This hurt my heart, more than the stroke of a switch,
that, where she was, her slave might not enter.
I shall be with her always as flesh on nail
and hear no word of blame from friend nor uncle.

Never the sister of my uncle
was loved of me so much, by this my soul.
For near as is the finger to the nail,
so please her, I would linger in her room.
So can love do with me, that in my heart enters,
his will, more than strong man with a frail switch.

*[213]*

Since the flowering of the dry switch,
or since from Adam descended nephew or uncle,
such love as that which now in my heart enters
has been, I think, in no body nor soul,
for where she is, in plaza or in her room,
my heart leaves her not by the length of a nail.

For her my heart is on a nail
and clings to her as tight as bark on switch.
For joy she is my tower, palace, and room
nor love I so brother, parent, nor uncle.
In paradise two joys shall have my soul
if there, for his true love, no man may enter.

Arnaut here sends his song of nail and uncle
for grace of her whose switch is as her soul,
to Desirat, whose fame all rooms may enter.

*[214]*

# FINNSBURG

*(From the Anglo-Saxon)*

Then there cried   out the king young in war:
"Neither dawn in the east   nor a dragon flying,
nor on this hall   the horn gables burning.
They bring on the battle;   the birds are singing;
the gray wolf wails;   the war wood thunders;
shield takes the shaft.   Now shines the moon
drifting in the cloud.   Death deeds are rising
that force upon us   this folk's hatred.
Wake you, wake you   my warmen all!
Holding your lindenshields   hard think on bravery,
bluster in battlefront,   bear you like men!"
     Rose many a gold-armed thegn   girding his sword on him;
doorward they made their way,   deadliest champions.
Sigeferth and Eaha   drew out their swords,
while at the other door   Ordlaf and Guthlaf
and Hengest himself   held it behind them.
     Guthere cried out now   to Garulf in warning
not to risk his frank life   on this first foray
hazarding his armor   against the hall door,
since one hard in fight   would have it from him.
But the daring hero asked   openly above all
who was the fighting man   holding the doorway.
"Sigeferth is my name," he said,   "Secgan my people;
a warrior wide known.   I won through many woes
and hard fighting.   Here now is fated
which of two things   you shall win from me."
     Then in the hall   was a huge noise of havoc
and the hard shields held   in the hands of the fighters
and the bonehelms burst   and the burgfloor echoed,
until in this grim fight   Garulf went under,
first man to fall   of the Frisian people,
Guthlaf's son with   good men about him,
many huge bodies.   The raven hovered

[215]

swarthy and gloom hued.    Swordlight stood forth
as if all Finnsburg    were flaming afire.
Never have I heard how    in heroes' battles
sixty battlethegns    bore themselves better,
how young men better paid    for the pale mead given
than his henchmen gave    to Hnaef at his need.

    Fought they for five days,    fell not a man of them,
none of Hnaef's henchmen    holding the doorways.
A wounded warrior went    back on his way then
and told how his battleshirt    was broken apart,
his warscarf no help,    a hole in his helm.
The king of the people    questioned him presently,
asked how the Danes    were enduring their wounds
and after the young men . . . .

*[216]*

# THE BLACK PANTHER

### (From Leconte de Lisle)


Pallors of rose widen across the clouds. The sky
along its eastern margin crinkles with fresh light,
and, in a shower of drops resolved, merge in the sea
    pearls from the necklace of the night.

Now all one quarter of the sky, sheathed in soft flames,
gathers to gold on the blue glitter of its spire.
One lingering fold, ablush against the green of gems,
    whelms all in dripping rain of fire.

And from bamboos that wake against the beating wings
of wind, and lichees purple-fruited, and upon
cinnamon trees where dews are bunched in glittering
    globes, swarm the fresh murmurs of the dawn.

From wood and hillside, flowers, from height of moss, along
the soft and subtle atmosphere, begins a flight,
from air suddenly troubled, of odors sweet and strong,
    fevered with promise of delight.

There, where all paths are lost in virgin growth of trees
and thick grass steams against the sun in morning glades,
by streams quick-running deep between declivities,
    beneath rattans in green arcades,

she goes, the queen of Java, the dark huntress. Dawn
sees her return to the lair, where her little ones
disconsolately yowl heap-huddled, one upon
    another, nested in shining bones.

[217]

Watchful, with eyes barbed like arrows, in sinuous stride
she walks among the glooms of heavy boughs, restless,
with fresh blood spattered here and there along her side
    and damp upon her velvet dress.

She drags with her a remnant of the beast she killed
and fed on in the night, quarter and half the back
of a grand stag. On moss and flower, grim traces spilled,
    red, wet, and warm still, stain her track.

Above, brown bees and butterflies, in rivalry
of play, flutter against and brush with wings the flow
of her back. Fronds in a thousand corbeils joyously
    perfume the ground where her pads go.

And, mail uncoiling from the middle of his red
thicket of thorns, to watch above surrounding grasses,
the python rears a flat and interested head,
    but keeps his distance as she passes.

Under the towering fern she slithers out of sight
without noise. The mossed stalks bend as she shoulders by.
Sounds fall silent; the air burns; the enormous light
    sleeps on the forest and the sky.

[218]

## DUM DIANA VITREA

*(Carmina Burana 37)*

When Diana, late at night,
for her crystal lamp reclaims
pink and paler light
kindled from her brother's flames,
western winds soft and fair
fill the air,
clear the sky,
and as by
music falling from above
cast their spell
and compel
hearts once hard to yield to love,
as the evening star again
bright and new,
fresh with dew,
charms to sleep mortal men.

O felicity
of sleep careless
that comes to set us free
from all distress,
and through the eyes' entry
making sweet ingress
prepares us for sorcery
of love's progress.

Morpheus, shaper in the mind,
brings us for dreams
soft blowing wind,
murmuring of streams
over clean sand running,

mill wheel sound
all night long turning
slowly round and round
softly to mesmerize
day-weary eyes.

After love's blandishing
and soft exchanges,
sleep comes languishing;
new strength outranges
all past sweet experience
and swims in new ecstasies of sense.
Lovely to sleep after love's strain,
but lovelier to wake from sleep to love again.

Under green trellises
where Philomela sings the lay
of her sad jealousies,
sweet to sleep the night away,
but sweeter still to play
with a girl in the grass,
and with such beauty pass
all the time away.

Smell of thyme and roses
and all things growing
gently disposes
of all our hearts' undoing,
and the heart in weariness
after love's commerces
softly reposes.

[220]

TWO SONNETS

*(From Joachim du Bellay, Les Regrets)*

### 31

Happy is he who like Ulysses has come home,
or like that hero who attained the Golden Fleece,
successful, full of knowledge gained, in sweet release
to live with his own people and no longer roam.
But when shall I behold once more the smoke arise
from chimneys in my little village street, and see
my own poor house and garden, which mean more to me
than a whole province, and look better to my eyes?
I take more joy in the retreat my fathers built
than Roman palaces with their facades of gilt,
and more than marble our good slatework pleases me,
better than Latin Tiber this French Loire of mine,
my little Lyré better than the Palatine,
sweet Anjou air more than the wind from the great sea.

### 79

I do not write of love, with no love on my mind;
I do not write of beauty, I have no sweetheart;
I do not write of sweetness, knowing only smart;
I do not write of pleasure, pain is all I find.
I do not write of luck, being unfortunate;
I do not write of favor, with my Princess gone;
I do not write of precious things, when I have none;
I do not write of health, knowing my feeble state.
I do not write of the court, far from my Prince's side;
I do not write of France, when I must wander wide;
I do not write of honor, for I see none here.
I do not write of friendship, which I find untrue;
I do not write of virtue, for I miss that too;
I do not write of learning, with the clergy near.

## THE FALL OF THE CITY

*(Three Songs from Euripides)*

### 1

Ilion, o my city,
no longer will you be named among the cities
never taken: lost in the Greek stormcloud,
speared, sacked,
your wreath of towers hacked
from your head: sorry, fouled
in the smoke and the ash strain,
sad city
I shall not walk in you again.

Ruin came at midnight.
We were in our room, sleep-eyed, happy,
tired, with the dancing over
and the songs for our won war,
everything over, my husband resting,
his weapons hung on the wall,
no Greeks to be seen any more,
the armed fleet
lost from our shores and gone.

I was just doing my hair
for the night, and the golden mirror
showed me my own face there
calm and still with delight,
ready for love and sleep.
And then the noise broke out in the streets
and a cry never heard before:
"Greeks,
Greeks, it is ours." (They said.) "Finish the war:
break kill burn:
end it, and we can go home."

Out of our bed, half naked
like any Dorian girl
I ran for the sanctuary
of Artemis' shrine. No use, for I never made it.
I saw my husband die.
They have taken me over the sea.
I looked back at my city.
Greek
ships hasten for home, taking me
with them, foredone
with sorrow and pity.

Curse Helen, curse
Paris, the fatal pair
whose love came too dear,
who married to destroy
my people my marriage and me,
whose marriage burned Troy.
May she never tread Greek ground.
I hope she never makes it over the sea.
I hope she is wrecked and drowned.
She ruined me.

2

Apollo, who built the strong towers of Troy on the hill,
Poseidon, who steer your black horses over the great gulf of the sea,
what did Troy do or not do
to make you turn your own handiwork over to the War God's will?

So many were the chariots you marshaled along the shore
and bloody sports of men where nobody won.
The kings of Troy are dead and gone,
and the fire on the altars of Troy shines through the fragrant smoke no more.

*[223]*

And Agamemnon is gone, dead by his wife's hand,
and she in her turn has paid the blood price and died,
killed by her children and the god's command.
The son stood in the holy oracular place with his mother's blood on him.
God, God, how can I believe it and understand?

Through the slave markets of Greece, many wives knew
fresh masters for their arms, as they mourned
lost homes and children. The pain, Andromache, came not only to you
and yours. Plague, plague was what Greece endured, but it crossed to the
      Trojan fields
in a drizzle of blood, Death's poisonous dew.

      3

Wind, sea wind
who skim the light swift ship
far over the sea,
what will you do with me?
In whose house will I be
as a slave bought and owned?
Somewhere in Dorian country,
somewhere in Thessaly
where rivers run so sweet?

Is it islands
where they are carrying me
to live my poor life out
where the Delian palm tree
and the laurel branched and flowered
for Leto's agony?
There with the Delian girls
shall I sing the mystery
of Artemis, veil and bow?

[224]

Or in Athene's city
of proud processionals
shall I work on embroidery,
or design horses and flowers
on intricate tapestry,
or scenes of mythology,
the fall of the Titan powers
stunned by thunder to sleep?

I weep for my children, weep
for my fathers' city
crumbled in fire and gone
in the smoke, war-won
by Greeks. I as a slave
in strange Greece shall live on
with a little Greek room of my own
for my grave.

*[225]*

HJALMAR

*(From Leconte de Lisle)*


A clear night and a frozen wind. Blood on the snow.
A thousand fighting men who all unburied lie
with sword in fist and hollow eyes. None stirs, although
above them ravens in black circles wheel and cry.

The cold moon scatters into distance her pale flares.
Hjalmar heaves himself up among the bleeding dead
propped with both hands upon a broken sword, and wears
the battle color on his flanks awash with red.

Hola! And is there one left among all those boys
so strong and cheerful, who still holds some scrap of breath,
you who this morning laughed and filled the air with noise
and sang like blackbirds in the closes of their heath?

They are all silent. And my helm is smashed, my armor
riven, the battle axe has knocked its nails away.
My eyes bleed. In my ears sounds an enormous murmur
that is like the clamoring of wolves, or of the sea.

Come over here, raven, my fine eater of men
and cram your iron beak deep in my chest. For here
we shall be waiting for you when you come again.
Carry my smoking heart to the daughter of Ylmer

in Upsala, where the jarls sit to their good beer
and sing in chorus as they clash their cups of gold.
With all your speed, o prowler of the heath, fly there.
Seek out my love and give my heart to her. High, cold

[226]

on the grand tower, where the blackbirds swarm and nest,
you will see her standing pale amid her long black hair.
From both her ears hang ear-rings, silver of the best.
Her eyes shine clearer than the stars in temperate air.

Go, my dark messenger, and tell her without fail
I love her, and this is my heart; and she will know
that it is red and strong, not tremulous or pale.
And she, Ylmer's daughter, will smile on you, Corbeau.

For me, I die. My life leaks out through twenty holes.
So drink, you wolves, this crimson blood. My time is done.
I free and fadeless, take my place among those souls
who join the gods, young, brave and laughing, in the sun.

[227]

# THREE POEMS FROM GÉRARD DE NERVAL

### The Dark Blot

He who has gazed against the sun sees everywhere
he looks thereafter, palpitating on the air
before his eyes, a smudge that will not go away.

So in my days of still-youth, my audacity,
I dared look on the splendor momentarily.
The dark blot on my greedy eyes has come to stay.

Since when, worn like a badge of mourning in the sight
of all around me where my eye may chance to light,
I see the dark smudge settle upon everyone.

Forever thus between my happiness and me?
Alas for us, the eagle only, only he
can look, and not be hurt, on splendor and the sun.


### El Desdichado

I am the dark, the widowed, the disconsolate.
I am the prince of Aquitaine whose tower is down.
My only star is dead, and star-configurate
my lute wears Melancholy's mark, a blackened sun.
Here in the midnight of the grave, give back, of late
my consolation, Pausilippe, the Italian
sea, with that flower so sweet once to my desolate
heart, and the trellis where the vine and rose are one.
Am I Love? Am I Phoebus, Biron, Lusignan?
Crimson the queen's kiss blazes still upon my face.
The siren's naked cave has been my dreaming place.
Twice have I forced the crossing of the Acheron
and played on Orpheus' lyre in alternate complaint
Mélusine's cries against the moaning of the Saint.

*Delphica*

Do you remember, Daphne, that archaic strain
by the sycamore base, by pale laurels, below
the olive tree, the myrtle or disturbed willow,
that song of love forever rising once again?
Do you remember that huge court, the god's domain,
those bitter lemons where the marks your teeth made show,
the cave whose rash indwellers found death long ago
where sleeps the seed primeval of the dragon slain?
They will come back, those gods whom you forever mourn,
for time shall see the order of old days reborn.
The earth has shuddered to a breath of prophecy.
And yet the sybil with her Latin face serene
lies sleeping still beneath the arch of Constantine
where no break mars the cold gateway's austerity.

*[229]*

VERGIL AENEID 1. 142—156


He spoke, and quicker than it was said made quiet the swollen
waters, and scattered the massed clouds, and brought the sun back.
Now Cymothoë and Triton aiding her worked hard to dislodge
the ships from the spiked rocks, while the god himself with his trident
pried them free, and cleared the vast shoals, and tempered the water,
then glided on wheels light and smooth on the waves' extremities.
As when in some great population incessant discord
has risen, and the heart in the vile rabble rages; now
torches fly in the air, and stones, fury arms them, but then
if perhaps they catch sight of a man who for merits and citizen's
worth has weight among them, they fall silent and stand with listening
ears; he speaks, and quiets their minds and softens their feelings;
so all crashing of the sea collapsed when the father of waters
looked out upon them, and riding under an open sky deflected
here and there his horses with slack rein and flying chariot.

*[230]*

Therefore Philippi saw once more the Roman battalions
clash upon each other with weapons matched; and the high gods
deigned twice over that with our blood the wide fields of Haemus
and Emathia be made fat and flourish. Surely the time shall
come when in those reaches the farmer following the plowshare
cramped to earth shall come on javelins thin with rust-rot
or with the weight of the mattock turn up hollow helmets.
Gods of our fathers grown to our soil, O Romulus, Vesta
mother and savior of Tuscany, Tiber, Rome's Palatine ridges,
deny not that this young man at least shall be healer
to our collapsed world. We have paid enough long since in our own
blood for the sins and the treachery of Troy and Laomedon.
Now long since the kingdom of the sky has envied you, Caesar,
us and you, is sick of bringing to pass the triumphs of mortals,
right sometimes and sometimes wicked; the world at warfare
so many times; so many faces of cruelty; never the farmer's
right he merits; the tillers swept away and the fields gone
foul, the curved reaping-hooks beaten stark into swordblades.
From the east Euphrates, from the north Germany stirs to battle.
Close cities have broken their links of peace and go armed now
for civil strife; the savagery of bloody Mars fills the whole globe.
As when chariots for racing have burst from their caverned
stalls, go wild abroad, and with vain hands clutching the guide-reins
helpless the charioteer is carried at the will of his horses.

*[231]*

# THE FIRST STEP

*(From Constantine Cavafy)*

One day, when Theocritus was at leisure,
the young poet Eumenes came to him
and said: "I have been writing now for two years,
and all I have done is one little poem.
That one poem is all my work so far.
But if I look high above me,
the stairway of Poetry is very high,
and from the first step where I am now,
how shall I ever climb it? I am so unhappy."
Theocritus said: "These words of yours
are discordant with the truth. They are blasphemy.
If you are on the first step,
you should be proud and happy in your fortune.
To have come where you have come is no small thing.
To have done as much as you have is a high honor,
and that first step where you stand already
is far from the world of ordinary people.
To have reached this step
you must be good enough to qualify
as a citizen of the city of ideas;
and it is hard to come into that city,
and few are inscribed among its citizens.
In its capital you will find magistrates
who do not smile upon any chance arrival.
To have come where you have come is no small thing.
To have done as much as you have is a high honor."

[232]

# NEW POEMS

REPORT FROM A PLANET

Those were countries simple to observe, difficult
to interpret. Young men are sage and bearded; grandmothers
are pretty; the married care little for marriage, but have

many babies; black and white were never so close and cordial,
and never hated so much; elder counsellors are brainless
but play good tennis. Their heroes, who are genuine

heroes, are also killers. These people can do anything
difficult, but nothing easy: catch and tame sight
and sound out of space; stroll in it; fly tons of steel

and come down on a handkerchief, yet can not realize a simple
covenant. Hundreds of wise men are united by subtle
communication, to form one mind and talk like a single idiot.

We have seen angels dropping fire on straw villages,
and fiends sentimentally entertained by pitiful
musicians imitating the entertainers of angels.

We have seen more good than ever we saw before
accomplishing unendurable evil.

We have seen a whole world ruled by a handful of men.
No two from one country.

*[233]*

# NOTES FROM THE ODYSSEY

*Elpenor*

The first young man ever to be called badly adjusted,
I suppose I was bored. We stayed too long, with the captain
wrapped up in his sweet blonde witch, the mate always cross

and complaining; the girls turning up their noses, and smiling
at the older men who had wives at home. Always it had been
like that: frightened of fighting, glad to be out of

the way: seasick easily, subject to blisters, indifferent
oarsman. Perhaps I'd have been more happy staying as another
pig among pigs? I did what I could. Circe's cellar

was open to all, and up on the roof with my bottle, watching
the stars, it all came out easy and sure, until I stepped
over that damned roof. The black crash of my neck. Nothing

remembered after that except blowing like a thin wind
over the sea: me, myself, but no body, hands or feet, nothing
but a draft, a dreaming direction: came to, to find myself facing

the captain across a ditchful of sheep's blood, telling him
(for once) I must have my grave mound and my oar, my name
and honor. At least, I had been part of that ship's company.

[234]

*Circe*

My forest night is padded soft with paws
and lit with yellow eyes. These monsters move
by stress of sightless leashes. So my bears,
my gentle wolves and leopards, whom I love
as a queen loves her slaves, nuzzle my hand,
move dark and silent up and down my stairs.
The night is full of the soft noise of fur,
and here before my doorstep every dawn
the lions open lazy eyes and yawn,
flex heavy paws, and purr.

My brainless dears, each fresh and seasonal maid
of the serving four, who lull my bath and bed,
has had her time of men and being undone
each night, and with each dawn renewed again.
The human beasts are gone. The heavy fauves remain.

It is long since those scarecrows came ashore
in reeking shirts, those frayed and frightened men,
their captain dogged in the events of war
and storm. Some were my beasts awhile, and then
restored, renewed. Dip in the beast, and serve.

A time of nights. Now men and time are gone
back to their sea of sharks and poisonous caves,
the splintered masts and the devouring foam
where, plagued with gods, the Mediterranean raves.
It is enough for Circe to stay home.
The pins of silence tingle in the air.
Look out and see the lions on my lawn
waken and stretch, yawn and benignly glare.
I love my beasts. I love my forest home.

*[235]*

*Penelope*

After my dream had drifted through the horn,
and in my sleep I lost my snowy skein,
I lay unconscious in the shuttered room.

No screams broke through the wall where men were torn.
I came from sleep radiant, as from a bath,
to my own hearth, and saw the man was there,

a strong stranger, my own heart gone to sea
those twenty years, pulled home by time's thin string,
all unfamiliar to be held awhile.

I heard the story of the bleeding room,
the rape of youth, the spirit like an owl
haunting the fight with rumor and gray wings.

Cherish my heart recaptured. It must surge
to love again, sweet unity, but how
shall I forget these things which have been done:

my faithless weeping maids with bucket and sponge
mopping the mess, then hanged all in a line,
my suitors stacked like cordwood by the wall?

I sent my suitors chits and promises.
I fed my tame geese milk and grains of corn:
my snowy geese, who now lie wrecked and maimed.

*[236]*

*Odysseus*

Happy is he who like Ulysses has returned,
and seen his housework done, the dead guests shoveled out
of the dining room into the street and burned,
the pretty maids all in a row strung on the line
like wash, and now, with the day clean, can look about
and say: I have come home. All this is mine.

The heavens and the hells I sailed between,
all the long days, are stored inside my skull.
They storm and stammer. Men's heads bob like crows
along the water, the girl-goddess throws
her sheet on a dead face. All is too full
of death. The bone-house too must be swept clean.

So, when I have planted my oar, I shall
not sail again. The gulfs are here, and all
enough to drink me down. I want no sea.
I have lived out the whole shape of mankind;
nothing of man but has been found in me,
and nothing left but live with my own mind.

Here is my wife (what is she like?), my son,
to comfort me for having all I prayed
to have. I wash the ghosts out of my head,
those moths, my moments; the girl-memories,
the tides, the teeth, the dreams are all undone.
Now I shall wash my hands and go to bed.

[237]

# SIRENS IN THE AEGEAN

This happened. Rowboat. Mid-day.
An old fisherman at the oars
and American passengers,
two girls, one man. The bay
blue, sun gay.

Too much for the girls, that blue
and gold. What could they do?
What could they do but stand
up, take off everything and go over the side
and paddle there, white hand
on the bow. The old man cursed them, crossed himself, and cried.

And the girls laughed, and the old
man sobbed and spat in the bay
and cursed the white hand on the bow.
Nereids drew him that day.
He hated it.
        Long ago.
They don't swim that way now.

*[238]*

MIRRORS


Speak back in looks.
Glass water steel
can bulb a double cloud, upend a tree,
or shape a face.

Truth, or likelihood.
Beauty can preen; this is an hourglass too,
rendering tired metabolism, times
of collapse in armpit and elbow, broken hair,
the salt hollow of the throat.
The sharper eye, the duller seen.

No compromise with station. Magnates, kings,
get back no quality, only tired men,
and break their mirrors.

Antique,
framed in ivory or silver, handled
in bronze, buried and found,
They catch up sight of faces, imitate
the imitation of faces long ago
now and forever dead;
once seen.

Sometimes it only means
the sky has fallen into the water.

Do mirrors also see?

[239]

Simulacrum of substance. The word, to be,
without third dimension;
but the is-not is caught and seen in the eye
that sees the eye, or I.

Unwindowed monad, private universe.

(Turning his back to the gorgon,
misting with breath
the pure steel, from what looks over his shoulder
one sees the frozen eyes, and does not freeze.)

By the redintegrated logic of sight
false made true truth falsified
the monster of unsight is seen and known.

These fictions are ourselves; all we can see.
The rest, these hills valleys and forests, these
owned and intractable topographies,
mirrorless are viewed from our steep angle, wrong,
ridiculous: no face, only the small
blurred promontory of the nose, and seen
cross-eyed: no back, no al-
together. Our own nude models are found
self-seen in glass.

The last philosophy of mirrors.

Two mirrors opposed
seal in, stitchless and seamless, infinite regress
in a drop of glass.

[240]

## DISLIKE OF TASKS

In sour seasons, in diff-
icult wind, stubborn snow,
handle the stiff
work, resistant thought, know

weight harder than force
hurting hands, the black
idea of failure. Your course
is one forward, two back.

Frozen, can't unlock it.
Sticks in the socket.

Material not made
for such use
fights needle and blade,
resists, or works loose.

In sour seasons, pursue
the impossible task, the year's
new repulse. All true
silk purses are made of sows' ears.
It's hard to do.

*[241]*

# THE SWARTHMORE PHI BETA KAPPA POEM

We are told of a white flower
secretly grown, divinely revealed. Once given,
it and its owner have a magical power
to defeat evil and death. And this is heaven-

bestowed wisdom, we are told. Do not be a believer
in wisdom as some herb to be possessed
by grace. She loves no favor.
Private but public, inward but expressed.

She has no secrets, no esoteric seal.
Is common and with us. She can not,
finding some garbage and filth in this real
world, therefore leave it to rot.

No hermitess, she lives calm in a storm
of sense. No mystic, she owns no shrine.
Reasons coldly out of a warm
perception. Is neither beastly nor divine.

Nor can art, philosophy, science own
such stature. She herself is her own last
degree, and stands alone.
All catch some gleam of her, and are surpassed.

So I see wisdom. Do not credit me.
Look at yourselves in your own worlds, and give
no trust to emblems or mythology
to find that wisdom in which you shall live.

*[242]*

# THE DAY

The tranquil lion and the confident lamb
came to the field and lay down side by side,
love filled the air, the world was strawberry jam,
the CIA and Cosa Nostra died,
the Arabs gave away their oil, Castro
and Rusk embraced publicly in the squares,
usury failed and national pride was low,
a band of angels played salvation airs.
Where had we ever missed our turn before?
Fascists were kind, and communists told the truth,
athletes and dancers made a game of war,
and immorality vanished with the pill.
That was when I recovered my lost youth.
Fish swam in trees and water ran up hill.

*[243]*

# FIRST FLIGHT

Sitting in the long corridor
and from behind glass
I watch the big ducks waddle out and pass,
open and close, spin roar
and turn, accelerate, lift, and soar:

and my number comes up (who? me?
Why did they spin
that bottle?) The goodbye kiss (hastily).
The walk (last?) Slammed door.
I'm sealed in.

(I'm brain stuff, I'm
the gray matter in the bone shell
I imagined, I'm
the population of my own tidy hell).

The map reels. Shake tilt and climb,
level and float
on fleece. I'm Wynken Blynken and Nod,
and my bed is like a little boat
(but it isn't a bed), or I'm
nearer my God to thee;
but why ever me?

(But angels do it dreams do it eagles do
it. But not stuffed like a fish
in a bottle, not as all one frail
old egg in one steel basket).

                              Now we sail
in cotton wool and muffle through
into clear sudden air,
and stare
and aim at the toy houses of a toy town,
miss the tops, bump lightly, wheel
in, open, and totter down
into a civilized field
populated and miles from everywhere.

# THE LAST TRAIN OUT OF WHITE RIVER JUNCTION

In the barren station, myself alone,
I sit and write
my diary on the stroke of one.
How much sleep tonight?

Train's in. The whole
crew's drunk. Obscenities
rock the dark. I roll
doubled up on a short seat. Amenities

are absent. Do I regret
the airport's nylon efficiency,
the sleek and terrifying jet?
No. Safety is sufficiency.
I like this bet-

ter. But my mind's
a mess of tired facts,
and I hurt, but pull the blinds,
and sleep, poleaxed,

in shirt and pants for an hour.
Then it won't work.
I need a shower.

They threw us off in New York.

[245]

# KRUPP'S ESSEN

Once shattered now rebuilt. Commend the city.
The avenues are wide. Even the air
tastes clean. The men are hale, the women pretty.
The glockenspiel chimes quaintly in the square.
The pride and style of quality are there
from those suave armorers who make the guns,
and see that they are used, who always were
the beneficiaries of our hates, who once
and once again, despising present loss,
the fall of chiefs, the battles lost and won,
while Vickers and Dupont looked kindly on,
shook hands with the Comité des Forges across
Sedan and Strasbourg, Vimy and Argonne,
the broken Rhine, and Dunkirk, and Bastogne.

*[246]*

## THE PLAYERS IN TIVOLI

Pagliaccio sitting in his chair
holds somebody else's baby. Harlequin
deposited it there
and danced away.
Behind his back, Columbine
smiling and late
slips home after her date
with the old portly gay
but well heeled bore.
That's all there is to say?
There isn't any more?

Except that Pagliaccio, who was Harlequin
once, with somebody else's baby
on his lap—who will wait and wait
for the fun to begin,
for his wife maybe
to come home from her date,
wait-
ing for Lefty, for the barbarians, for the Robert E. Lee,
or perchance for the evening mail,
or even for the spark from heaven to fall
or possibly fail—
could never resemble you or me.

And except that Harlequin—who will some day be
Pagliaccio, who slipped
somebody somebody else's baby,
this limber masked stripped-
down model who dances on his toes,

[247]

usher and pimp, entrepreneur
of loveless loves, this elf,
fairy perhaps, voyeur
not greatly interested himself
in more than his own dance steps and his lines—
could never have planted babies or stolen Columbines
on or from anybody like us.

Except that Columbine, who will never be
anybody's grandmother, whose only function in life
is forever to be
the lovely loveless wife
and see
that her Pagliaccio is properly abused,
she, desired, dispassionate, forever seduced,
what is she to you and me?

The show has little wisdom and is not new,
is trite and mannered, does not consort with the times,
is only a tinsel, a rout of paperdoll mimes.
Trouble is, it's all true.

*[248]*

# ATLANTIC

They saw the island. It was perfectly plain.
Four signposts said that it was equally far
from New York and Southampton, and again
the distances to Iceland and the Azores
were equal. They could see a restaurant bar,
a radio station and a green golf course,
a monastery and a grammar school,
a cinema and a church, and in the street
green and red traffic lights, a swimming pool
with beach umbrellas, bikinis, a place to dance.
If it came from the bottom, it came complete.
In any case, the captain of the France
said to the captain of the Queen Mary: "That's queer.
I didn't remember there was anything here."

[249]

## THE LOVELY SWIMMERS

Diving for wrecks or sunken treasure, see
them, or for spoil, or delight and sweet ease
of the skin: boy, girl: silently
carving the deep underseas

illuminated fluid and color-change:
see them double, turn in a rapture
of quiet and pure form, arrange
by flight and pensive pursuit their capture

of motion in water: see them, purged
by immersion in liquid calms, pursue
the upper light and, with dark heads emerged,
decorate, those lovely swimmers, the bright blue.

*[250]*

## THE FLOWERING MEADOWS

Our sessions could be bleak in that small office
through sterile numbers, a desert of guesses
that never gave; with too many coffees
that killed no yawns in our long idlenesses,

sitting cross, counting failures like sheep,
until some germ took life, some min-
iature miracle, like an omen in sleep,
achieved the combination, and let us in

on the meadow, and suddenly the waving
crests were lush, and we went waist deep in absolute
luxury, reaping, raving,
and the ripe keys fell like fruit.

Comfort for barren hours,
for the long dry daydreams uninvolved
with answers. Once and again we found flowers.
Some problems get solved.

*[251]*

# IN MEMORIAM

*Elsie Campbell Sinclair Hodge, AB 1897.*
*Born Dec. 15,1874. Died in the massacre of Christians*
*at Paotingfu, China, June, 1900.*

This is the stone bench on the Bryn Mawr campus.
Sometimes in mild weather I teach my classes
at the bench of Elsie, killed by Chinese Boxers.

Mobs, rage, weapons. The sleeping dragon shook
his scales between the spells before his last
awakening to red fire and howling guards.

The quaint and pretty graduating class,
round-eyed before the camera, gave her up
to her short duties, love, and violent death.

The Empress Of India, small, yacht-prowed,
reeling in high waters off the Aleutians
(those stormy gray ships on the Eastern Grand Circle),

carried my parents, innocent and clever,
squeezed by hard means from their own academe,
to China, months and dollars away from home.

Where Elsie's blood was only six years faded,
at the hired temple, next the lily pond,
I was born in Paotingfu. The stars are joined.

All taught. It's in our blood, a hard gray strain
to discipline our little furies, knot
our stormy-colored lusts into cool form

until dragons shall dim their fires and smile.

[252]

# ATLANTIS NOW

They have their drowned dominion, cities made
of coral, sand, and wet stone, silences
where hand in hand the sunken cherubs promenade
the seamless miles between pelargic trees

of weeds waving, and helmed and armed in shell
the sea-knights swim on their improbable quest,
design inanimate combats, and dispel
the soundless tumults of their soft unrest.

Their sessions are water, bloodless argument
unseals a ghost of purpose in their state;
marriage of minds and blends of thought invent
the shapes that these blue realms incorporate.

And at small tables by their cavern door
the old myth makers, in gray hats and pale
raincoats, deliberate the ocean floor,
assess, drink coffee, and compose the tale.

*[253]*

## REPORTS OF MIDSUMMER GIRLS

Friends said: about eight o'clock they used to come
and call us to our windows, at eight, when light
was still enough to see by. Nice girls, but some
were lonely, and would come up and stay the night,

they said. And others said, by the Starnberger See
the waitresses swimming beneath the pier
would giggle and call up to us and play
hide and seek with us and murmur, wir sind hier,

so those friends said. And in the crowded night
girls gone or gray are calling to my friends
who now are gray or gone, to share the light
of lost long days before midsummer ends.

*[254]*

# ANDROS: WALLS AND LANES

Small blackish flat stones are laid
one on another. Dry walls
hold weather and wind, made
with ten foot intervals
for heavy stones set upright.
Huge flags have been laid between.
Stone lanes promenade the bight
and slant of the island scene.

Grubbed gathered and set by hand,
the stoneways promenade
length and breadth of the land.
Millions of motions made
them. Hard muscles of men
knotted like oak; the slight lift
of childish hands; careful women
piled stone: walls and ways, gift

of the people. Grace from all
this gone invisible strength
has patterned with lane and wall
the whole of the island length,
a monument put together
by millions of motions lost
and gone into wind and weather
of the island coast.

[255]

## JOURNEYS WITHOUT END

Who was that man in the story, lost his mate
in Orvieto cathedral (I think her name was Sally)
when her tourist party claimed her, and his date
with the hospitable huge letto matrimoniale

he had arranged stayed empty? How many Romeos
happened to miss Juliet's party, how many
contented separate Francescas and their Paolos
never read the book together. Oh, had any

but the almost impossible chance obtained,
what fragmentary we's could never meet,
but must, with fabulous others, have remained
lost in the crowd, forever incomplete.

*[256]*

# WHEN WE WERE YOUNG

The long hot mileage in a rusty car,
the dewy silos in the scrambled fields,
the sordid coffee at the counter-bar,
the absent-minded doves across the shield,
the eider quilt soaked in the meadow grass
the wayside sandwich from a paper sack,
the shrunken billfold and the slipping gas,
the question, will the patched tire last us back,
the town memorials of wars long ago,
the skyscraper huge as on a shoreless sea
the tranquil boats in ponds too short to row,
late love, sweet irresponsibility,
two in the world and the world all for two,
and poverty and health and I and you.

*[257]*

# THE LAKE ISLAND OF IANNINA

Without Iannina this island would have no identity.
It needs and has a small city near, to get away from.
Iannina drapes her shores with mosques minarets and clock towers,

clean streets and sordid alleys, filigree shops and barracks
and too many policemen. She guards her gray lake with memories
of Ali Pasha, of repression and murder, the drowned Greek women.

But the island across the water lies becalmed in reeds,
water forests secreting snipe coots and godwits.
At the corner grows a minute stone and plaster paved village.

Avenues are cut through the reeds for their boat landings.
Everyone has a boat protected by tiny breakwaters.
They fish and seine the lake, and serve the visitor

frogs if desired, brown crisp sections of eels, crayfish
scarlet and like infinitesimal lobsters with claws
surpassing their inch-long bodies. It is true

there was murder and treachery here, a century and a half
ago, but violence sleeps in the waters of tradition, charmed
into a ceremony of sentimental pictures, false stories

of true love. Rather, what is escape more than a remote
island in a remote lake? What if the postman steps
from the boat with a bag half full of air mail envelopes

from relatives in America? Strands to the outworld
are almost invisible. Gray reeds sheathed and filmed in gray water.
A small world of minute specialties hides in the reeds.

[258]

# TRANSCEND

Loose end ash of fire
windrow of cut grass
pluperfect of desire,
all is is was

unless outside of me
some voice is heard
wherever two or three
are gathered. Oh, third

self other
than stolid same I,
master teacher brother,
come. If grain must die

and not below
ground, to be born again,
let this grain know
at least it was grain.

*[259]*

# THE AGE OF ARMIES

Ravenna was an all-star battle; it had Bayard
and Gaston de Foix; miracles of address and valor;
but it was Alfonso d'Este, Duke of Ferrara,

who at last confounded the sinewy Spanish swordsmen
as Gaston plunged and died. Victory meant little,
so we are told, to Italy or to anyone.

So at Pavia, François was foiled by Austrians,
and the ringing battle-names succeed and star
such streets as Paris would have, Rivoli, Marengo,

Napoleon's own Lodi and Arcola. Italy got everybody
who was anybody, Swiss, Germans, those Austrian Spanish
or Catalans, one incredible ferocious old Russian

who knocked down a Scotch Highlander who was leading the French.
Who did what, yes, but for whom, in whose cause?
                                        Where oh where are
the silk and wool spinners of Lombardy, the corn-growers

of Po's plains, the Venetian, the Genoese fishermen?
They are locked behind their shuttered windows (Alps
were a useless barrier) waiting for the barbarian

invaders to be done with their prodigies of valor, pick up
their ghastly toys and go home, ever since the last armored Italian
achieved his unprofitable glory at the bridge of Ravenna.

*[260]*

## POEM FOR THE INAUGURATION OF HARRIS WOFFORD

*Bryn Mawr College, 1970*

In a time when our beloved possessions are turning against us,
when all are haggard with doubt, and the wisest counsels confounded,
when the natural world, once strong and sovereign, begins to strangle

on its own garbage, what are we, with moderate
wit and less wisdom, to offer even a morality, no program?
Only whatever sense of things stirs in the dark blood's tumult;

To cultivate what's difficult. To put aside dreams
of do-nothing paradises. To heal the haters, not hate them.
To forego our given luxuries of easy thought and spoiled senses.

To liberate the oppressed from the tyrannies of nature
and us. To make exacting use of magnificent material,
when asked for much to give more, and try to undo the sorrows

of ourselves and the sorrowful around and among us.

*[261]*

## SOLID POLLUTION: I

Oh ravishing corruptions from within.
How can we clear our channels, can we breathe
among our own confections now, when skin
and bones are all we carry outwards. Underneath
a sky that swarms with fury, guarded tight
by grudging bulks that sit there, rot and crumble
(cast-off containers of our once delight),
physical glory's excrements now humble
the pride of spirit in a brain unfed
by blood that strives through its own fats to reach
the starving monarch, our material head.
We need our props, but by their use impeach
our sovereignty. We spoil what we live by
by merely living. Through that life we die.

*[262]*

THE FORT

On a hill top two or three
men with light weapons, awful food
and scant water, resignedly
waited for whatever likelihood

they waited for: raids scouts foreign
attack. A rudely piled tower
of cut stones served as warren
to hide in from sunlight power

dews, and their little events ensued
and vanished into lost time. Weather
and time collapsed their tower, their rude
masonry became ruder stones in heather

and holm oak, and with more time the stones
assimilated themselves to the hollow ground
contours of the hill's natural bones.
A shape of an idea of men and fort can be found

with good will and imagination today.
Unrecorded history is that way

*[263]*

## BATHERS CHANGE

On Greek beaches Greek girls behind a screen
of white chemise and the crossed arms of friends
change and emerge to bathe (nothing being seen
in the former process).
The young man's skivvies are his bathing dress.

In Michigan Connecticut and Maine
dark damp well-labeled, proper and opaque
partitioned rooms inhibit and constrain
the changing male and fe-
male in their separate respectability.

In the blond north and Scandinavian night
discriminate sexes may go frankly bare,
while by our temperate waters Aphrodit-
e in a bathing suit
rules her boardwalk as sovereign absolute.

(But what can take away the feel of sand
on toes, of boards on heels, the glimpse and drift
of water, warmth of bare hand laid on hand,
or, sheltered and close by,
white change slipping the corner of the eye?)

Custom can have its custom. I like best
our days, and our own ways, where by sea, lake,
or mountain torrent we undressed and dressed
behind some kind of wall
of modesty, or ferns, or nothing at all.

*[264]*

# WHEN YOU ARE OLD: AFTER RONSARD

When you are old, you will sit late and spin your wool
by candle light beside the fire, and you will say,
as you admire these verses that I make today:
"Ronsard praised me, when I was young and beautiful."
Then each of those old servants who attend your days,
dreaming and half asleep for work and weariness,
will start up when they hear you say Ronsard, and bless
your name for being given such immortal praise.
I shall be underground, a disembodied shade
lolling among the myrtles of the shadowy glade.
You will be an old crone huddled above your grate,
regretting my lost love and sorry for your scorn.
Trust me, live now, do not await tomorrow's morn,
but pluck life's roses now, before it is too late.

*[265]*

# MY PAST LIFE

*From the French of Charles Baudelaire*

I lived for a long time beneath vast particoes
colored by the marine sun into infinite
fires, and their tall pillars, majestic and upright,
turned them with evening into basaltic grottoes.

The sea's waves, rolling the reflections of the skies,
mingled, in solemn music and deep mystery,
the overwhelming chords of their rich harmony
with all the sunset colors mirrored in my eyes.

It was there that I lived among voluptuous calms,
surrounded by blue seas, by splendors and by waves,
and by my naked, fragrantly perfumed slaves

who cooled my forehead, fanning me with leaves of palms,
whose sole appointed duty was to read and know
the secret of that sorrow which oppressed me so.

SONNET

*From the French of Felix Arvers*

My soul contains a secret mystery all its own,
a love born in a moment which will never die.
I have not spoken, since all hope has passed me by,
and she, the only cause of it, has never known.

Oh, I have passed close by her, and she did not see.
Always alone, although forever by her side,
I shall live out my time on earth, until I have died
without ever asking, and with nothing given to me.

Although God made her so compassionate and dear,
she will go by, lost in her thoughts, and never hear
the love that where she goes murmurs on every hand.

Devoted to her austere duty, she will say
reading this verse so full of her in every way:
"Who can this woman be?" And never understand.

*[267]*

## "SHE HAD THIS WAY"

*From the French of Victor Hugo*


Ever since she was very small, she had this way
of coming to my room to visit every day.
She was the ray of light and hope I waited for.
She said: "Good morning, little father" at the door,
came in, opened my books and worksheets, took my pen,
sat on my bed, laughed at the mess, went out again
all of a sudden like a passing bird. Then I,
feeling refreshed and lighter in the mind, would try
to write once more, and as I wrote would often see
among my manuscripts and drafts of poetry
some wild and weird design or other she had made,
or unused sheets of paper that her hands had frayed.
Somehow or other my best verse was written on these.
She loved God. She loved flowers, and stars, and living trees.
Though she was no grown woman she was witty and wise,
The radiance of her soul was mirrored in her eyes.
She asked me about everything she wanted to know.
We had those shining winter nights, we loved them so,
discussing language, literature, and history,
my wife near, my four children clustered by my knee,
all friends there by the fireside. That was how we spent
our times. We had so little, and how much it meant.
To think that she is dead! Oh, help me now, dear God.
I never could be gay when I thought she was sad.
All festive evening outings left me cold, if I
had seen her looking wistful when I said goodbye.

*[268]*

# THREE POEMS BY PIERRE REVERDY

## The Skin of the Heart

We went down hill laughing through the trees
Along the road there was a ruined wall
From time to time
There were glimpses of other people
And there are houses not far at all
We shall not be left alone

Passing the house which was too low and had no stairs
Going ahead of those who turned back one by one
We sang

But something else was waiting for us farther on

Often we had to go back to that place
The door was closed
And that sad silly face
That frightened us

There is someone whom I have left behind
I find myself alone with people whom I cannot name
Nor can I now remember why I came

I have changed in voice and face
and those who knew me once no longer know me now
The sun goes watery in drops of rain
Where the brute wind has slammed a window pane
We had looked full upon each other you and I
And bit by bit I feel my shadow fade and die

*Heart Bell*

The bell that sounds and no one hears
The troubled air
The footstep heard upon the stair
No one comes in
And no one wants to come

There is a trembling shadow over there
The house is washed by evening on the window pane
I am alone
And the waiting-time
Has tied hour to year

Now there is nothing left to separate life and me
I do not want to sleep again
The dream is vain
I wish no longer now to know what's happening
Nor what I think
Nor who I am

In the night the pale walls dissolve around the stove
As the cat stared at signs upon the ceiling
This evening there will be
Nothing stop your memory
No one will come to see you

The heart better stifled now beats
Beneath the sheets
And struggles on in vain
Who will come to bestow
The final blow
So that it will never wake again

[270]

*In the Alien World*

I can no longer see your face
Where are you hiding
The house has disappeared among the clouds
And you have left the final window now
Where you used to appear
Come back what will become of me
You leave me here alone and I am full of fear

Remember the times when we walked side by side
Walking along the streets between the houses
And on the road lined
By bushes either side
Sometimes the wind would silence us
Sometimes the rain would make us blind
But you would sing in the sun
And the snow made me gay

I am alone I rub my eyes
I almost want to cry
We must go on through the shadow toward that light
There is a whole story to recall
The life so simple and so straight without all those little matters of detail
Do not hurry wait
Who is breathing here
When I am there who will be breathing too
But I dare go no further without you

Now I go to bed
Possibly for the sleep that never ends
Upon the couch where I was made to lay my head
Without ever learning more of life
I have forgotten all my friends
Several sweethearts and my family
I have slept winter and summer through
And in my sleep no laziness was found in me

But for you who have called me back again
I must get up again I know
Let us go the good days are over
The long nights that shorten so
When one sleeps as a lover

I waken to the full glum
Sound of a voice that is not human
I must go on walking I drag you away
To the dull sound of the drum
All the world is laughing at my sorrow
I must go on walking one more day

On the errand never done
When the hangman comes with his noose
Tonight the good days are gone
A thick voice calls for you
And for you the earth has grown cold

I see your face from afar
But I have not found it again
As I approach it is gone
From the window that is shut
You and I will not walk again

[272]

## THE ROSE

*From the French of Pierre de Ronsard*

Come, darling, let us go and see
whether that rose, who gorgeously
this morning opened to the sun
her colored robe, in these late hours
has lost the radiance begun
in her complexion rivalling yours.

Oh, no! How in this little time,
see, darling, she has lost her prime
No, no! Her beauties left to blight,
o jealous nature, we must grieve
when such a flower as this can live
only from morning until night.
Then, if you will believe me, dear,
this little while your youth is here
in its most green and flowering pride,
pluck and enjoy what's yours to spend
before old age can come, to end
beauty, as for this rose who died.

*[273]*

## PIERRE RONSARD AND HIS ROSE

Speak, Peter Ronsard. Did she do
everything that you asked her to?
I hope for your short life that she
was kind, and in some garden close
between the sunlight and the shade
you caught and kissed your young French rose.
Yet some, more fortunate than you
and she, hold till gray age the charms
of married roses in their arms,
grown lovelier as their years go by.
I know some flowers that never fade
until, as flowers must do, they die.

*[274]*

## DATE DUE